RAILWAYS AROUND WHITBY
VOLUME ONE

Scarborough – Whitby – Saltburn, Malton – Goathland – Whitby, Esk Valley, Forge Valley and Gilling Lines

Martin Bairstow

Published by Martin Bairstow, 53 Kirklees Drive, Farsley, Leeds
Printed by Amadeus Press Ltd, Huddersfield, West Yorkshire

Railways Around Whitby

Volume One

This is an enlarged and updated edition of *Railways Around Whitby* which first appeared in 1989. To avoid extensive resetting, most of the original text has been left unchanged with additional material added where appropriate. Almost all the original photographs are retained but some have been rescanned to give a better result.

Thanks are due to everybody who has given help and material. The maps were drawn by John Holroyd as were the gradient profiles from information supplied by Patrick Howat. The excursion leaflets and tickets are from the respective collections of David Beeken and Geoffrey Lewthwaite. The photographs are credited individually.

Sadly, it will not be possible for me to deliver copies of this new edition to John Bateman nor John Halliday. Both contributed to the original book but have since passed away. Volume Two carries a dedication to John Bateman. A similar tribute to John Halliday will appear in a forthcoming book.

Volume Two

First published in 1996, this explores some aspects of the story in greater depth.

Readers may gauge that I did not quite see eye to eye with the philosophy behind the closures of 6 March 1965. But what could I, as a then 12 year old schoolboy, possibly have known about the real world facing railway managers in 1964/65? That was the question posed by John Oxley in an otherwise complimentary letter which he sent after publication of Volume One in 1989.

So for Volume Two, John and I tried to look deeper into the reasons why Whitby was left with only an indirect rail link via Middlesbrough. We conclude that, if Whitby was to retain only one railway connection, then the Middlesbrough line was indeed the correct one to save. Other themes are introduced by guest contributors. David R Smith explains how one could travel cheaply, if at some discomfort, on an early morning return. Chris Wilson records his journey by the last train over the Forge Valley Line. Andrew McRae fills in some further detail on camping coaches. Jim Warnes tells us of his days as a signalman at Prospect Hill. Freda Phillips looks back to her childhood in the station houses at Staithes and Glaisdale.

Richard Pulleyn describes his role in demolishing the Malton to Grosmont line. He didn't succeed entirely as witness the 20 pages devoted to the North Yorkshire Moors Railway. Bill Smith visits Whitby and Middlesbrough engine sheds whilst Anthony Silson recalls holiday journeys when the full network was still in operation. Having missed the last train from Scarborough to Whitby by some 31 years, Stuart Baker and I bike it instead.

All this and more. The book is fully illustrated with photographs and line drawings which are all different from those appearing in Volume One.

A8 4-6-2T No.69854 approaching Sleights with the 12.40 Middlesbrough to Whitby Town via Battersby in August 1957. *(A. M. Ross)*

Introduction

To my regret I did not journey to Whitby by rail until 1969 and must therefore confess that I never travelled on any of the closed sections of line featured in this book.

Twice during 1964 I purchased a 'Day Line' ticket covering the southern half of the North Eastern Region. I saw the Whitby dmu in the bay platform at Malton. The ticket would have covered it and many of my alternative but discarded itineraries would have included it. Instead, on both occasions, I stuck virtually to the lines which are still open.

Although I was very young, I knew what was going on and what was threatened but I could not comprehend how quickly and how brutally the threat would be carried out. In 1964 it would have even been possible to find an excursion train to Kirbymoorside. By the following year the 'Day Line' ticket had been abolished but a day return to Bridlington had become sufficient to cover virtually all the surviving railways along the Yorkshire Coast.

Compared to many seaside resorts, Whitby may be said not to have fared too badly when the axe fell. It depends whether you live south of York or north of Darlington. From either point of view, an enormous gap appeared in the railway map depriving us not just of quaint country branch lines but of lines which would have had a future in an age of sprinters, senior citizens railcards and incurable road traffic congestion.

The book begins with a tale by Stuart Carmichael about a railway service now long vanished. The history is then traced of the four main routes out of Whitby: to Malton, Middlesbrough, Saltburn and Scarborough and for completeness there is mention of the Forge Valley Line which used to connect Scarborough with Pickering. Inclusion of the Ryedale lines may appear to be drifting some way from Whitby but it gives the opportunity to link up with 'Railways Around Harrogate' at Pilmoor and demonstrates how the present dead end at Pickering was not just a through station but an important junction.

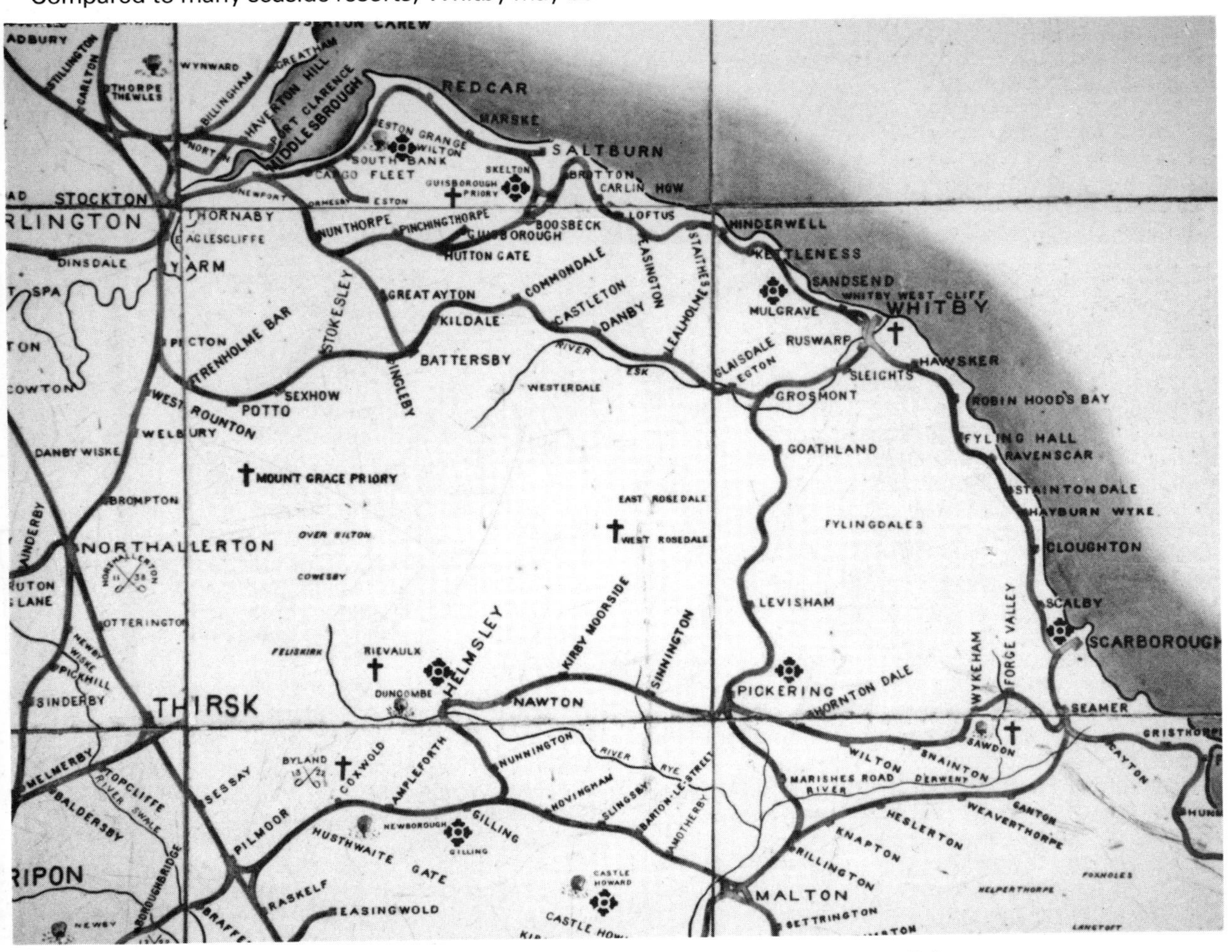

A section of an NER tile map, in this case the one at Beverley Station, serves as an introduction to 'Railways Around Whitby'. The layout at Malton is not quite correct! *(John Bateman)*

Camping at Sandsend

by Stuart Carmichael

The Bay at Sandsend showing the three camping coaches at East Row and the two at the station.
(Tindales of Whitby)

In the late 1950s and early '60s most of our holidays were taken in Camping Coaches, which were ideal for a family of extended proportions as one rarely had to lug suitcases, spades and yachts more than fifty yards from the station. My father was a railwayman at that time and the privilege fares were an essential feature of the holiday budget.

I believe our first Camping Coach holiday was in 1957 at Sandsend, almost certainly in May to take advantage of the low season rates. As a ten year old I had no idea that people would do anything as pointless as spending a day at a station collecting locomotive numbers but I was sufficiently stirred by Leeds City's 'Midland Compounds' and the gleaming brass foxes on the nameplates of 'Hunts' to note their numbers in my first diary.

Little remains in my memory of that holiday except sun, sand, sea and a train ride from Sandsend to Staithes: an all-too-short fifteen minutes clinging to the cliff edge, thundering up the 1 in 57 through Sandsend Tunnel to re-appear apparently suspended in mid-air before plunging a few seconds later into Kettleness Tunnel. The pungent smell of smoke and the mellow dustiness of wooden carriages never fail to re-kindle that early excitement. It was something of an anti-climax to have to spend four hours in Staithes at high tide until the return train.

May 1958 saw a repeat visit to Sandsend. We left the bitter cavernous gloom of Leeds City at 9.22 am behind 'Hunt' class No. 62765 'The Goathland'. If we had just been heading for Whitby, we could have changed at Malton where the 11.00 to Whitby Town was waiting in the bay platform, but that would not have enabled us to reach Sandsend. This explains why we took the longer route via Scarborough. A single change here put us on to the 11.40 direct to Sandsend.

The winter timetable offered just two through trains from Scarborough to Middlesbrough, at 11.40 am and 4.24 pm. There was in addition a morning train starting from Whitby Town at 7.00 for Middlesbrough and an evening one at 7.40 from Scarborough to Whitby. Normally these trains would have comprised just two coaches, which meant that they could be propelled out of Scarborough station to avoid the engine having to run round at Falsgrave Junction.

This, however, was no ordinary day. Our train was in fact the penultimate northbound working over the superbly scenic route between Whitby and Loftus. In anticipation of the occasion drawing additional traffic,

Complete with brass fox nameplate, 'Hunt' class No. 62769 'The Oakley' draws out of Scarborough Station on 31 August 1952. Falsgrave Tunnel is on the left. *(John Oxley)*

the load was increased to five bogies, which meant that the train had to depart from Platform 1A. This was bad news for my parents, who had to make the extra trek to the far end of Platform 1 in the hope of finding a compartment for our party of seven.

My memories of the journey behind Standard 2-6-4T No. 80116 are vague but are supplemented by a report in the August 1958 edition of *Trains Illustrated* by Mr K. Hoole, who was covering the event from the footplate.

We left Scarborough three minutes late as was normal practice when Platform 1A was in use. As soon as the engine had cleared the points leading on to the Whitby line, we changed direction and plunged into Falsgrave Tunnel. At that time the first section of line was regulated by track circuit block, so it was not until Gallows Close box that we picked up the first single-line token.

After achieving over 40 miles per hour, we were forced to slow down for the 30 mph restriction through Scalby, where the station had closed in 1953. Trains did still call occasionally to deliver customers to the four camping coaches which occupied the station yard. Further coaches were positioned along this route at Cloughton, Stainton Dale, Ravenscar, and Robin Hood's Bay.

Our first station stop was at Cloughton, where we exchanged tokens. Although on the winter timetable we were not booked to pass another train until Loftus, the greater volume of summer traffic required that this labour-intensive ritual be carried out at all the passing loops en route.

On leaving Cloughton we began to climb. Over the next five miles the gradient was to stiffen from an initial 1 in 90 to 1 in 71 on the pull out of Hayburn Wyke and finally 1 in 41, covered at just under 20 mph, from Stainton Dale to the summit at Ravenscar. As soon as we set off from Ravenscar we began to coast down the 1 in 39 overlooking the sea towards the small station at Fyling Hall. Here the porter dealt with a couple of passengers and then locked the station, which was henceforth to become unstaffed, and joined the train himself.

Leaving Robin Hood's Bay, we were again struggling to maintain 20 mph on the 1½ mile climb at 1 in 43 from which one could now enjoy a view back towards Ravenscar. Once over this next summit, it was a steady drop through Hawsker and over Larpool Viaduct until we reached Prospect Hill Junction, where we joined the line out of Whitby Town for the final climb up to West Cliff Station. Here we took water and changed crews.

Once away from West Cliff it was only six minutes to Sandsend. First we descended at 1 in 60 across the viaducts at Upgang, Newholm Beck, and East Row, by which time we were virtually on the beach, then we began to climb again over Sandsend Viaduct and into the station. Here we were met by the Station Master, Mr Goodall, who later presented us with a 'last ticket' as a souvenir of what must have been a sad day for him.

We had arrived at 12.44 and a southbound train went through at 1.48. The next pair of trains would be the last. After spending part of the afternoon acclimatising ourselves to the Camping Coach, we returned to the platform where a small crowd had gathered to witness the passing of the 5.28 train for Middlesbrough.

This, the 4.24 from Scarborough, headed by class L1 2-6-4T No. 67754, was booked to pass the last southbound train at Kettleness. This was the same set upon which we had travelled, still in the care of 80116. It was two or three minutes late due to the antics of a press photographer who had nearly missed it at Kettleness.

As soon as the last train drew to a halt at Sandsend, carriage doors were flung open and the platform filled with running photographers. The mayhem was con-

80116 on a Scarborough to Middlesbrough 'express' waiting to pass a southbound train at Staintondale. *(N. E. Stead Collection)*

80118 disappears over Sandsend Viaduct with the 9.25am Middlesbrough to Whitby Town on the final day of service. *(David R. Smith)*

A superb holiday setting. Sandsend station with camping coaches in 1957. *(J.C.W. Halliday)*

A small crowd waits to greet the arrival of the last northbound train at Sandsend on 3 May 1958, the 16.27 Scarborough to Middlesbrough drawn by class L1 2-6-4T No. 67754. *(Tindales of Whitby)*

cluded when the same gentleman of the press, determined to get the best shot, refused the door held open for him by the Station Master and tried to board the last carriage. He misjudged the acceleration down the 1 in 62 over Sandsend Viaduct and was left behind. After that there was a feeling of emptiness, although the lack of trains in the following days did bring new opportunities.

The highlight of the previous year was being allowed to pull off a signal in the tiny Sandsend cabin, but now we were free to clamber across the track and make a direct, if precipitous, path down to the beach. Sandsend boasted two sets of green and cream Camping Coaches – a pair at the station and three at East Row which were virtually on the beach and a more attractive proposition to us lads. East Row was always booked up well in advance and we never got in there; I suspect my parents were glad as it would have meant a ¾ mile walk from the station back towards Whitby.

My overriding impressions of a Camping Coach were the sense of space and light, the heavy brass handles, leather window straps, and the smell of paraffin for lamps and cooker. We climbed along running boards, hid among bogies, fought over the top bunk and were fascinated by the window blinds. We learned from grandfather how to find rabbit runs, set a snickle, and kill and skin a rabbit. There were guinea fowl roaming alongside the track towards Hinderwell and we searched fruitlessly for their eggs. Our morning chore was to fetch water from the station in immaculate examples of the tin-smith's craft: oval-sectioned containers with close-fitting lids and wire handles.

At the end of the week it was a disappointment to have to return to Whitby by bus, but the DMU to Scarborough was a new experience. Having lost the coastal line through Sandsend, we did at least have the compensation of the better view afforded from the new trains over the equally spectacular coastal stretches of the Scarborough and Whitby line.

The following year we stayed in a Camping Coach at Goathland, but by then I had been initiated into the rites and delights of train-spotting at Rothwell Grammar School, about a mile from Ardsley shed. The lack of sea and sand no longer mattered on holiday, as long as there was a railway outside the door, with the thrilling spectacle each afternoon of a B1, usually 61002 'Impala', rushing non-stop through Goathland in a swirl of smoke and stream on the 5.53 pm to Malton and York. Our holiday this year must have been in high summer as this train only ran from the beginning of July to the end of August.

Steam was still supreme in 1959 and if there were a few DMUs they were not noted. A grimy class Q6 0-8-0 would clank through with the pick-up freight, a far cry from the highly polished T2 No. 2238 which graces the North Yorkshire Moors Railway today. One of Malton shed's pair of Standard Class 3 2-6-2T's, No. 82029, was a regular performer that summer, its

The last train to call at Sandsend, the 17.44 to Scarborough in the care of 'Standard' 2-6-4T No. 80116.
(Stuart Carmichael collection)

determined performance up the 1 in 49 from Beckhole to Goathland signalled well in advance by its rasping exhaust and attendant plume of steam and cinders. The regulator used to remain open until it reached the start of the platform in contrast to the two 'Black Fives' and GWR 0-6-2T which shut down well before the station in the summer of 1988, when I had the pleasure of a week in one of the NYMR Camping Coaches at Goathland.

In 1959 we were woken at 6.12 am by the 5.20 from Malton, but today one can enjoy a more civilised start to the day, the first train arriving from Pickering behind the Class 25 at 10.40 and awaiting the arrival of the steam-hauled train from Grosmont a couple of minutes later. I was pleased to see a different locomotive on this turn each day that I was there and I would think that only an arrival at Ingrow, on the Keighley & Worth Valley Railway could match the awesome power of a steam-powered entry to Goathland.

Our journey to Goathland was inevitably by car which was also essential for excursions. Travelling to Whitby for the day by train would have involved lengthy waits for 'connections' at Grosmont. It seems a poor strategy on the parts of BR and the NYMR to cut themselves off from the potential market in Whitby and I think the sooner that the NYMR can run through to Whitby or BR can provide real connections the better.

The current Camping Coaches at Goathland are converted from Mk. 1 stock and have better facilities in terms of cooking, washing, seating and WCs than the old coaches, but the bunks, which are laid transversely, are not as comfortable as the properly built wooden longitudinal bunks of the previous style. Heating and fire safety are vastly improved from the 1950s, when paraffin and wood panelling were the norm. Safety at Goathland has also benefitted from the installation of the footbridge, which I was pleased to see does not detract from the appearance of the station and looks as though it has always been there.

By restoring the camping coach facility, the NYMR has continued a feature of the railway scene which has almost been forgotten. The preservation of Goathland Station would have been incomplete without it.

The last campers had already gone when this view was taken at Goathland on 6 March 1965—until the NYMR restored the camping coach facility.
(G.W. Allenby)

More on Camping Coaches

From an LNER advertising leaflet, a view of the camping coaches at the south end of Robin Hood's Bay Station.
(David Beeken collection)

Stuart Carmichael's story has prompted a deeper look into the subject of camping coaches. Assistance came in the form of advertising material in the collection of David Beeken and a feature on LNER camping coaches by C.S. Carter and A.A. MacLean in 'British Railway Journal No. 23' published in 1988.

In June 1933, the LNER hastily adapted ten old Great Northern six wheelers and placed them at the disposal of holiday makers on ten branch lines. The conversion was so crude that initially there was no gangway access between the living quarters and the sleeping compartments.

According to the first publicity, the coaches could be booked at any one of a number of listed stations on the particular line and could be moved, on request to the Station Master, to a different station on the same branch during the course of the holiday.

In 1933 there were four coaches in the Whitby area which were offered for hire as follows:

Esk Valley:
At Kildale, Castleton Moor, Danby, Lealholm or Glaisdale.

Yorkshire Coast (Scarborough-Whitby):
At Cloughton, Stainton Dale or Robin Hood's Bay.

Yorkshire Coast (Whitby-Loftus):
At Sandsend, Kettleness or Staithes.

North Yorkshire Moors:
At Goathland or Levisham.

Campers were warned that some stations such as Kettleness were remote from shops and other amenities but were advised that the Station Master, 'their best friend' would buy in provisions by prior arrangement. All linen, crockery and kitchen utensils were provided. Water and conveniences were available at the station. Access into the coach was by ladder unless it happened to be parked in a platform.

The initial scheme was a success and over the next few years the number of vehicles was increased and the standard of them improved. The LMS Railway copied the idea in 1934. By 1938 coaches were available in the Whitby area at:

Staithes	Coxwold
Kettleness (2)	Helmsley

Sandsend (2)
East Row (3)
Robin Hood's Bay (3)
Ravenscar (2)
Staintondale (2)
Cloughton (3)
Goathland
Levisham
Kirbymoorside
Forge Valley
Thornton Dale
Glaisdale (2)
Castleton Moor
Danby
Lealholm

Helmsley lost its allocation for the 1939 season. The facility to move the coach elsewhere up the branch had been withdrawn but the 1939 brochure offered the 'Touring Camping Coach' giving a week's holiday starting from York. The coach travelled by ordinary passenger train and spent three nights at Pateley Bridge, two at Aysgarth and two at Glaisdale. Alternative or longer itineraries were available by negotiation. The coach had six single sleeping compartments plus living room, kitchen and toilet and was available to individual parties of at least six people.

Camping coaches were painted in the same green and cream livery as LNER tourist stock and Sentinel railcars. It was always a condition of booking in both LNER and BR periods that the journey to the campsite was undertaken by rail.

Inevitably the Second World War put a stop to the business which was not resumed until 1952 when BR converted a number of ex Great Eastern eight wheel non corridor coaches. The number of locations was fewer. There was no deployment in Ryedale or the Upper Esk Valley whilst the Forge Valley line had been closed.

After closure of the Whitby to Loftus route in 1958, its coaches were redeployed so that the main allocation was on and around the Scarborough to Whitby line. In 1963 coaches were located as follows:

Robin Hood's Bay (5)
Ravenscar (2)
Stainton Dale (2)
Cloughton (3)
Scalby (4)
Ruswarp
Grosmont (2)
Goathland

The concentration at Robin Hood's Bay and Scalby may have been due to the availability of electricity. Elsewhere bottled gas was used for lighting, heating and cooking.

Scalby Station had closed to regular passenger traffic on 28 February 1953 after which part of the station building was made available as a camping cottage. Trains continued to stop on summer

Pictured at Claughton in 1934, No.42082 was a Great Northern six wheeler of 1885 vintage.
(Andrew McRae Collection)

An LNER publicity photograph taken at Forge Valley which played host to a camping coach each season until 1939. *(Andrew McRae Collection)*

Saturdays for the convenience of camping coach and cottage patrons. Hayburn Wyke Station was also used as a camping cottage.

1964 was the last season during which camping facilities were available on the North Eastern Region of British Railways. The only four coaches outside the Whitby area were at Bolton Abbey, Newbiggin on Sea and two at Hornsea. By the spring of 1965, these stations had suffered the same fate as those on the Scarborough–Whitby and Malton–Whitby lines. Camping coaches lingered on for a few more years on other BR regions.

Even if routes like Scarborough–Whitby had survived, it is unlikely that the camping coaches would have lasted if only because the stations at which they were sited would have become unstaffed. In an age of growing private caravan ownership, customers would not have been satisfied for much longer trotting off to the station loo. The primitive facilities would have had to be improved and staff would have been needed specially to service the coaches, presumably on a year round basis with full railway conditions of employment. What had started as a cheap facility might have ended up costing more than a package tour to the Mediterranean.

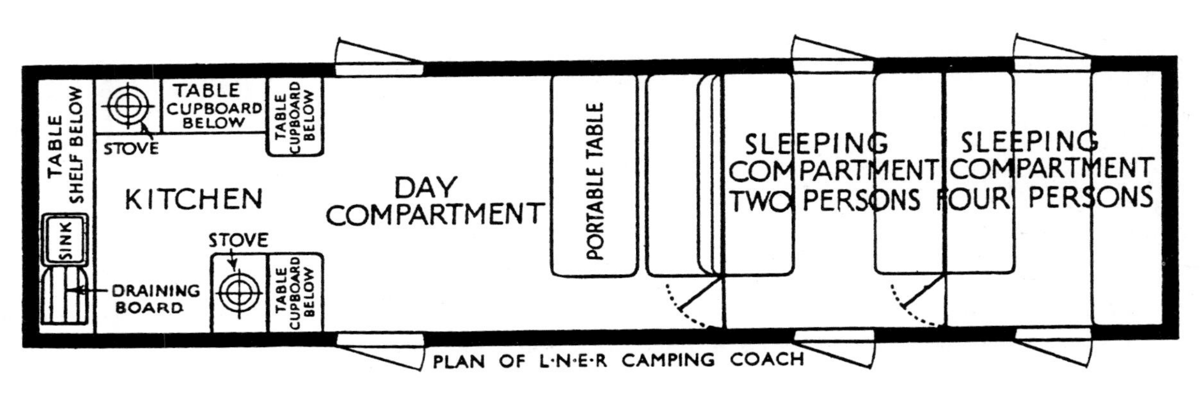

PLAN OF L·N·E·R CAMPING COACH

The Whitby & Pickering Railway

The story of Railways Around Whitby predates the main thrust of railway expansion by a good twelve years. When the Act for the Whitby & Pickering Railway was passed in May 1833, it was for a purely local venture which stopped short of making full use of technology which was available even then. It was to be a low cost line for horse power only with probably no thought of it ever becoming part of a national system of railways.

At that stage the only existing railway in Yorkshire was the Stockton & Darlington which had been extended to Middlesbrough in 1830. The idea of a railway connecting Whitby with the Stockton & Darlington was rejected by George Stephenson on the grounds that it would not be able to compete with coastal shipping. The function of railways was to put the interior of the country in communication with the ports.

Stephenson favoured the Whitby & Pickering project which was to cut through the very difficult terrain between the coast and the Vale of Pickering. If goods could be conveyed that far by rail, then onward transport by road was just about practicable.

It was whilst working on the project, that Stephenson the engineer made the aquaintance of George Hudson the entrepreneur who happened to be visiting some inherited property in the district. The association which followed this chance meeting was to play a major part in determining the shape of the future rail network. It also ensured that George Stephenson would not in future need to be bothered with enterprises as small as the Whitby & Pickering Railway.

The main engineering features of the railway were the nine crossings of the River Esk between Whitby and Grosmont all on wooden bridges, the castellated tunnel at Grosmont and the rope worked incline between Beck Hole and Goathland 1500 yards in length at a maximum gradient of 1 in 10. 'Motive power' was achieved on the self balancing principle. The descending train was always heavier than the ascending one by virtue of a water tank which could be filled from a reservoir at the top and then emptied into a stream at Beck Hole before being dragged back up to the top by a team of horses.

A trial run was made between Whitby and Grosmont on 15 May 1835 using a carriage called 'Premier'. This was basically a stage coach on flanged wheels. Six passengers could sit inside, four outside at the front, another four at the back and a few on top. The driver sat on top and a guard seems also to have been employed. A public service operated over this first six and a quarter miles of the railway from 8th June 1835.

The railway was completed throughout in time for formal opening on 26 May 1836 although there may have been some traffic carried to Pickering prior to that day. An account of the celebrations was written by Thomas Clark, Esq, the Treasurer of the Railway and published in 'The Scenery of the Whitby & Pickering Railway' by Henry Belcher. Crowds assembled outside the Angle Inn, Whitby, in good time for the procession to the station which began at 7.30 am to the accompaniment of the Whitby Brass Band.

There appear to have been at least six carriages available to guests and these were drawn individually by horses. At Grosmont the party paused to admire the lime kilns under construction – a development which was attributed to the advent of the railway. Another promising source of traffic was the Whitby Stone Company beyond Grosmont and the guests were treated to a demonstration of a wagon loaded with stone being lowered down an incline from the hillside quarry. At Beck Hole the horses were detached and the passenger vehicles, which had been coupled together, were hauled up the incline at 'a pleasing, rapid and easy pace'.

A fresh set of horses then took over for the next

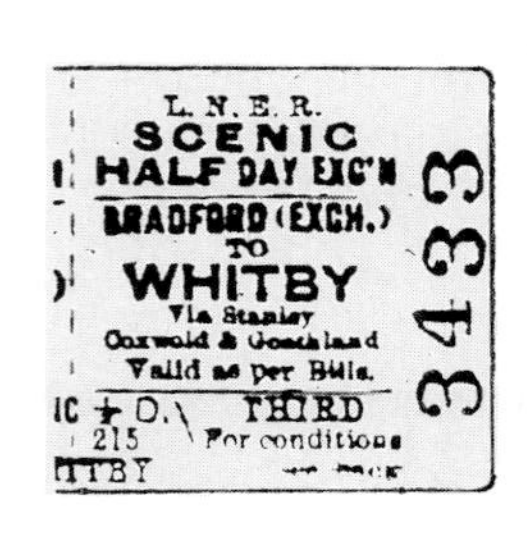

A8 4-6-2T No.69865 at Whitby Town in the mid 1950s.
(D. Ibbotson collection)

stage to the summit of the line. In normal working the horses might then have earned themselves a ride in a dandy cart attached to the train before resuming their task at the point about four miles short of Pickering where the gradient became insufficient to proceed any further by gravity. On the opening day the horses were left behind at the Summit and the carriages, coupled together, were allowed to reach a speed of 30 mph on the downgrade if Mr Clark's report is to be believed. A fresh team of horses completed the last leg of the journey into Pickering where a band was waiting to escort the party to the Black Swan. Here they 'sat down to a most excellent déjeuner à la fourchette.'

Highlight of the return journey occurred during the descent of the incline when passengers were given a demonstration of the precision with which the guard could stop the train 'in the midst of its rapid downward course'. Arrival back in Whitby was at 5 pm. Guests then returned to the Angel Inn where the celebration went on until two the following morning.

The railway then settled down to an every day existence. There were normally two passenger services each way daily except Sundays. 'Bradshaw' for 1844 shows the principal departure from Whitby at 8 am. This took about 2½ hours to Pickering whence a stage coach went on to York there to connect with main line trains which had been able to reach that City from London and the Midlands since 1840. A second 'luggage train' at lower fares left Whitby at 2 pm and was advertised to reach Pickering at six. In the other direction the 'luggage train' left Pickering at noon. Passengers on the 'express' service left York at midday in order to catch the 3.30 pm from Pickering which brought them into Whitby at six.

Compared to what had been possible before the railway, the above arrangements were revolutionary but by the mid 1840s the pace of the Whitby & Pickering Railway was rapidly being overtaken by developments elsewhere. Horse operation was not only slow but very labour intensive. A horse could only pull one vehicle and it was necessary to 'double head' on the long up grade from Raindale to Goathland Summit.

Whitby loco shed was built in 1868 to replace an earlier Y&NM structure dating from 1847. It provided motive power for all four routes radiating from Whitby but closed with dieselisation in April 1959. G5 No. 67330 and A8 Nos. 69864 and 69865 stand in the shed yard on 3 September 1952.
(John Oxley)

NER class X3 2-2-4T No. 1679 outside Whitby Shed on 25 June 1919. Built as a tender engine in 1860 and rebuilt in 1894, the loco was described as an officers' special tank engine. It survived until 1931.
(LCGB, Ken Nunn collection)

A Whitby to Middlesbrough dmu passing under Larpool Viaduct in 1966. Weeds have begun to take over the Scarborough line which climbs up the embankment on the left from Bog Hall towards Prospect Hill Junction. *(D.J. Mitchell)*

A Goathland to Whitby dmu calls at Ruswarp early in 1965. Today there is just the right hand platform remaining. The buildings have been sold off and the signal box has vanished. *(D.J. Mitchell)*

Sleights Station in 1968. The view is towards Grosmont. *(D. Butterfield)*

Grosmont Station looking through the tunnel towards Deviation Junction Box. The original small tunnel for horse drawn traffic is to the left but obscured in this 1950s view.
(J.C.W. Halliday)

Deviation Junction box marked the divergence between the 1865 'main line' and what became the branch to Beck Hole. This is now the site of the NYMR loco sheds.
(G.W. Allenby)

Class J25 No. 65671 surmounts the 1 in 49 climb up to Goathland Staion with a southbound freight on 1 August 1951. *(D. Butterfield)*

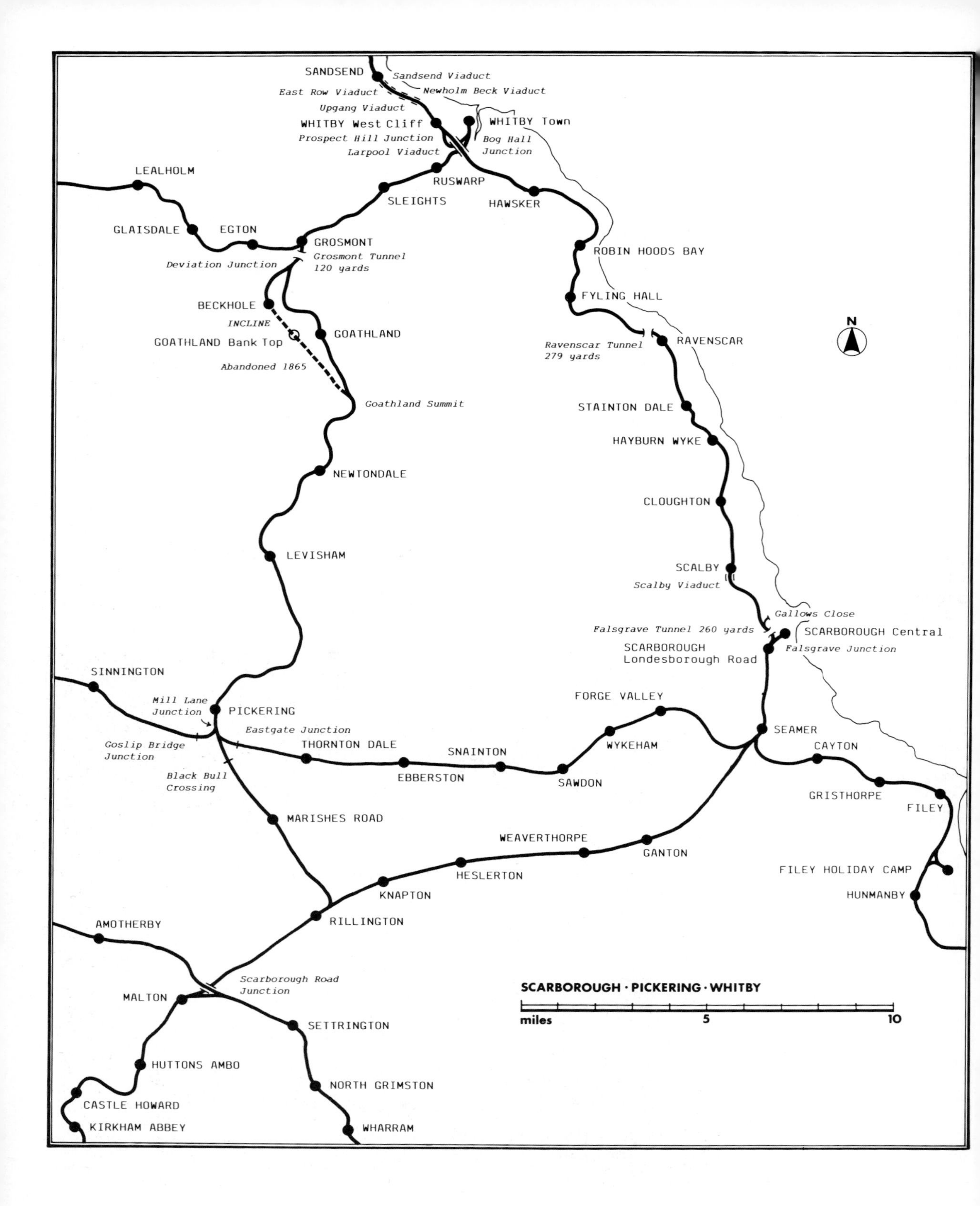
SANDSEND
Sandsend Viaduct
East Row Viaduct
Newholm Beck Viaduct
Upgang Viaduct
WHITBY West Cliff
WHITBY Town
Prospect Hill Junction
Bog Hall
Junction
Larpool Viaduct
LEALHOLM
RUSWARP
SLEIGHTS
HAWSKER
GLAISDALE
EGTON
GROSMONT
ROBIN HOODS BAY
Grosmont Tunnel
120 yards
Deviation Junction
BECKHOLE
FYLING HALL
INCLINE
GOATHLAND
GOATHLAND Bank Top
Ravenscar Tunnel
279 yards
RAVENSCAR
N
Abandoned 1865
Goathland Summit
STAINTON DALE
HAYBURN WYKE
NEWTONDALE
CLOUGHTON
LEVISHAM
SCALBY
Scalby Viaduct
Gallows Close
Falsgrave Tunnel 260 yards
SCARBOROUGH Central
SCARBOROUGH
Londesborough Road
Falsgrave Junction
SINNINGTON
Mill Lane
Junction
PICKERING
FORGE VALLEY
Eastgate Junction
SEAMER
Goslip Bridge
Junction
THORNTON DALE
WYKEHAM
CAYTON
SNAINTON
EBBERSTON
SAWDON
Black Bull
Crossing
GRISTHORPE
FILEY
MARISHES ROAD
WEAVERTHORPE
GANTON
FILEY HOLIDAY CAMP
HESLERTON
HUNMANBY
KNAPTON
AMOTHERBY
RILLINGTON
Scarborough Road
Junction
SCARBOROUGH · PICKERING · WHITBY
MALTON
miles
5
10
SETTRINGTON
HUTTONS AMBO
NORTH GRIMSTON
CASTLE HOWARD
KIRKHAM ABBEY
WHARRAM

The York & North Midland Railway

This Hudson enterprise, as its name suggests, was formed to link York with the North Midland Railway at Altofts Junction just north of Normanton. Its completion on 1 July 1840 placed York at the end of a continuous railway from London and the Midlands. The York & North Midland Railway became a part of the North Eastern Railway in 1854. By that time it had extended to Scarborough, which George Hudson predicted would be turned into the 'Brighton of the North' and it had also ended the isolation of the Whitby & Pickering Railway. Hudson also had plans to develop the town of Whitby. In 1847 he started the Whitby Building Company which acquired some fields at West Cliff and started to cover the area with streets and terraced houses. Hudson's downfall in 1848 ended his personal involvement in the development of Whitby which was probably retarded as a result.

The railway from York to Scarborough with its branch to Pickering was authorised on 4 July 1844 and opened within the incredible space of one year and three days. This feat would not have been possible if the company had opted for a tunnel through the Howardian Hills but it chose instead to let the line meander with the River Derwent for nearly four miles. It is this which provides the York to Scarborough line with its main scenic attraction albeit at the cost of a long 45 mph restriction.

A week before the arrival of its first train in Pickering, the York & North Midland Railway obtained Parliament sanction to take over the Whitby & Pickering Railway which it proceeded to purchase for about three quarters of what it had cost to build. Over the next two years, the horse worked line was rebuilt with double track of heavier construction to take steam locomotives. Bridges were rebuilt in iron, a new tunnel was bored at Grosmont, some of the worst curves were eased and the hemp rope used to operate the incline was replaced by a steel one driven by steam power.

Steam operation began throughout to Whitby in July 1847. A loco shed was built at Beck Hole to house the engines at the northern end of the line which, once they had been lowered down the incline, tended to stay semi permanently to work that section.

The incline was an impediment which the North Eastern Railway took steps to overcome in its Act of 11 July 1861. This authorised a deviation line running for 4½ miles from a point south of Grosmont Tunnel to rejoin the earlier route just short of Goathland Summit. The new route opened on 1 July 1865. Built mostly on a 1 in 49 climb, it included a new station at Goathland. The old line was abandoned apart from the retention of a single track between Deviation Junction and Beck Hole. This was used to carry freight, mainly coal, to the isolated community at Beck Hole right until 1951 when a road was built. In 1908 a Summer only passenger service was re-

A scene which anticipates the preservation era: 'The Great Marquess' at Goathland on 13 April 1964 with a filming special. *(G.W. Morrison)*

introduced between Whitby and Beck Hole but it ceased on the outbreak of the First World War.

A curve east of Rillington off the Whitby line towards Scarborough was opened on the same day as the deviation to permit through working between the two coastal resorts albeit by a fairly circuitous route. The 1½ hour journey evidently failed to generate sufficient traffic so the curve only lasted for just over a year. It was then removed even though some years were still to elapse before construction of any more direct route between Whitby and Scarborough.

'Bradshaw' for April 1910 shows a winter service of six trains each way over the Whitby & Pickering line. Departures from Whitby Town were at 7.22, 8.35 and 9.15 am and at 12.10, 3.50 and 7.00 pm. All ran to Malton where connections to York were generally quite reasonable. Some trains were shown as only stopping by request at Marishes Road. On a Sunday there was just one train at 6.00 pm which was in fact the only advertised train from Whitby by any route on the seventh day. The corresponding inward working was at 6.10 in the morning from Malton.

The basic year round service never differed greatly from the pattern described above. At closure in March 1965 there were five trains each way plus two workings between Whitby and Goathland. There was no service on Winter Sundays. It was during the summer months that the line carried additional scheduled trains and excursions. Traffic built up in the 1930s as holidays and day trips to the coast became affordable by more people. A list of train departures from Whitby in the summer of 1938 appears on page 72.

The section of track between New Bridge, north of Pickering, and Levisham was singled during the First World War to free the materials for military use. The second track was never put back.

Why not remains a mystery which Graham Reussner, NYMR archivist, attempted to probe in the summer 1996 edition of *Moors Line*. With the help of research by David R Smith, he came to a possible, but by no means definite, answer.

A Metro Cammell twin car set drifts into Goathland in February 1965. *(Charles Allenby)*

Goathland Summit was a block post in BR days. It was at one stage planned that the North Yorkshire Moors Railway should terminate here. *(D. Ibbotson collection)*

During the First World War, the railways remained in private ownership but were controlled by the Government through the Railway Executive Committee. During 1916, the Government decided that the Army needed track so it requisitioned some little used sidings and even sections of running line where double track could, temporarily, be reduced to single.

Sunday 31 December 1916, a full engineering possession was taken between New Bridge and Levisham. Points and interlocking were disconnected, electric tablet instruments installed and by late afternoon single line working had been established over the former down (northbound) track. The up line was then removed. The intermediate signal box at Farworth was a casualty of the singling.

A similar thing happened between Speeton and Bempton on the Scarborough to Bridlington line and between Enthorpe and Southburn on the line from Market Weighton to Driffield. In both these cases, double track was reinstated about 1924 with the aid of compensation from the Government.

Redoubling from New Bridge to Levisham seems also to have been intended by the LNER at the same time but it was not carried out.

A possible explanation has been found in a memo dated 27 October 1923, according to which the Government compensation was £6,000, or about 10%, short of the cost of reinstating the three sections of line. Evidently, not all of the lifted track had gone to the front. Some had been used by the Railway itself for renewals.

Perhaps the LNER concluded that, if they had to meet part of the cost themselves, redoubling New Bridge to Levisham was not worth it. So the five mile section remained single, with electric tablet working, until closure in 1965. Today the NYMR operates it on the more primitive staff and ticket system.

Richard Pulleyn reminds us that staff and ticket working was also available between Mill Lane Junction (Pickering) and Rillington from the 1940s until the passenger closure in 1965. If the up (southbound) track was required for wagon storage then normal double line block working was suspended and traffic worked over the down line in both directions. Richard remembers the staff and ticket equipment at Mill Lane and the king lever which changed the method of working, but he recalls double line block actually being in use. The summer 1964 timetable shows no ordinary passenger trains booked to pass on the section though there was one moment in the day when it would have been very tight at Rillington if the 4.08pm from Malton had been forced to await the 4.04pm from Pickering coming off the branch.

There was a facing cross over at Mill Lane Junction, installed in 1924 to allow access onto the Gilling line when Goslip Bridge Junction was abolished (see page 59), Malton bound trains could thus cross on to the down line and then go back via the trailing crossover at Rillington.

A number of other lightly used sections of double track were worked as single lines either temporarily or permanently to make room for wagons storage including Picton to Ingleby (see page 36).

For the final 16 months when Pickering was open for freight only, the 'branch' from Rillington was worked with a 'one engine in steam' staff on the down track only.

A three car Metro Cammell dmu with parcels van in tow crosses onto the single line as it pulls away from Lewisham, bound for York in 1964.
(John Birkbeck)

The driver of a York to Whitby dmu picks up the single line token for Levisham at New Bridge Box in the Summer of 1964. *(John Birkbeck)*

The 8.55 am Whitby to Malton service remained steam hauled because it was the return working of the early morning mail train. B1 4-6-0 No. 61049 enters Pickering Station on 13 April 1964. *(D.J. Mitchell)*

The 11.00 am Malton to Whitby dmu pulls into Pickering on the last day of service, 6 March 1965. *(G.W. Allenby)*

Six Pickering signal boxes. From top left: New Bridge *(D. Ibbotson),* High Mill, Bridge Street, Hungate and Mill Lane Junction *(John Bateman)* and Eastgate Crossing on the Forge Valley Line *(Martin Bairstow).*

Black Bull Box controlled the crossing over the Malton road south of Pickering. 'The Great Marquess' heads towards Pickering with its three coach special on 13 April 1964. *(G.W. Morrison)*

Marishes Road Station looking towards Whitby.
(G.C. Lewthwaite)

The 11.00 am Malton to Whitby passing Marishes Road in August 1957. *(M. Mitchell)*

Malton Station looking east in August 1965. Communication between the two platforms was by means of a rolling bridge.
(John Bateman)

North of Whitby

The Stockton & Darlington Railway

Railways came early to Teesside. The Stockton & Darlington, the world's first public railway, was opened on 27 September 1825. It was extended along the Tees to Middlesbrough in 1830, Redcar in 1846 and to Saltburn in 1861.

The present diesel service which runs hourly from Bishop Auckland and half hourly from Darlington through Middlesbrough to Saltburn uses the original Stockton & Darlington line for part of the journey. At the time of its amalgamation with the North Eastern in 1863, the Stockton & Darlington extended into Weardale and across the Pennines to Tebay on the West Coast Main Line. Its territory also included the line to Guisborough which provided the first link in establishing a railway from Middlesbrough towards Whitby.

The Middlesbrough & Guisborough Railway

The Pease family had been instrumental in establishing the Stockton & Darlington Railway and the port of Middlesbrough. In the early 1850s they purchased the rights to mine ironstone at Cod Hill, near Guisborough. They then persuaded the Stockton & Darlington to lend its support in the promotion of the Middlesbrough & Guisborough Railway. This was authorised by an Act of June 1852 but there was difficulty raising the required share capital until Messrs Pease stepped in with an offer to guarantee the dividend.

The ten mile line opened for goods traffic on 11 November 1853. It was double track and included the climb at 1 in 44 for 1½ miles between Ormesby and Nunthorpe. A passenger service was introduced in February 1854.

The mine at Cod Hill was served by a branch which climbed at 1 in 54 from Low Cross Junction, east of Pinchinthorpe, for a distance of just under a mile. Then trains had to be drawn up a rope worked incline to reach the mine itself. The branch was short lived closing about 1865 but this apparent set back did not prevent the development of traffic from numerous other mines which opened in the Guisborough area between 1850 and 1880.

The Guisborough line was worked by the Stockton & Darlington which found itself in the enviable position of serving both the ironworks of County Durham and the sources of the iron ore in Cleveland. It was a logical step for the S & D to consolidate its position by absorbing the Middlesbrough & Guisborough Railway in 1858 on terms which guaranteed the M & G shareholders a dividend of 6% per annum. Many small railways were forced to sell out to their larger neighbours on far less favourable terms. Such was the importance of the iron ore traffic which soon tempted an alternative railway to try and break the S & D monopoly.

The Cleveland Railway

This was a rival line running more or less parallel with the Middlesbrough & Guisborough then continuing towards Loftus. It was backed by the West Hartlepool Harbour & Railway Company which hoped to gain a stake in the lucrative iron ore traffic south of the Tees by means of a ferry to carry wagons across the river to link up with its own system near Port Clarence.

Despite strenuous opposition from the Stockton & Darlington, the Cleveland Railway was incorporated by an Act of July 1858 but was authorised only to build the section east of Guisborough. The House of Commons Committee advised the promoters to link up at Guisborough with the Stockton & Darlington whom the Committee felt sure would afford every possible accommodation for Cleveland traffic otherwise it would be open to the Cleveland Railway to make a fresh application for an independent line.

The imposing exterior of Middlesbrough Station in 1968. The white building above the wine merchants, which was out of character, has now gone and the whole area has been stone cleaned. *(D. Butterfield)*

Guisborough Junction box where the Nunthorpe and Redcar routes diverged.
(John Bateman)

North Eastern railway 'BTP' 0-4-4T No. 87 sandwiched in the middle of the 2.42 pm 'autotrain' from Middlesbrough to Saltburn via Guisborough and Brotton ascending Nunthorpe bank on 24 April 1919. The additional vehicles in the rear will probably be detached at Guisborough.
(LCGB, Ken Nunn collection)

Guisborough Station looking towards the buffer stops from a Scarborough to Middlesbrough train. *(J.C.W. Halliday)*

Not content, the Cleveland came before Parliament the following year with a new bill claiming that circumstances had changed and that they needed to get direct to the Tees at Normanby in order to load ships with iron ore for export. The new Bill was passed by the Commons but defeated in the Lords. Their Lordships did however offer the advice that a private line might be built without an Act to take ironstone from the Eston area to the Tees.

Under the title of the Upsall, Normanby & Ormesby Railway, such a private line was staked out down to a pier on the Tees at Normanby. In August 1860 the Tees Conservancy Commissioners, who appeared to share the Stockton & Darlington's distaste for the new intruder sought an injunction on the grounds that the pier would be a hazard to shipping. The court failed to agree whereupon the Conservancy adopted an alternative method of opposition.

On 10 September the Conservancy hired an army of barges which it positioned so as to prevent work on the pier but the Cleveland Railway recruited its own hands to break the moorings and send the barges away. The space intended for the pier was then enclosed by chains attached to large buoys and the same fleet of barges was bought off to come and protect the Cleveland works. During the night the Conservancy 'forces' sailed down the river in three steam tugs intending to damage the works which they expected to be unprotected. Hardly had they got started than they were attacked by the same barges who had been on their side in the morning. After some fighting, the three tugs were driven away in a shower of stones, slag and lumps of iron.

In November 1860, the owner of Guisborough Estate, who was also one of the promoters of the Cleveland Railway, began work on a private line across his land supposedly to carry his own traffic onto the Upsall, Normanby & Ormesby Railway. In truth his purpose was to complete the link to the Cleveland Railway at Guisborough. The Stockton & Darlington asked the court to prevent a bridge being built over their line outside Guisborough Station but without success.

It only remained for the Cleveland Railway to apply to Parliament to turn these bits of partly constructed private railway into a public concern. Still under protest from the Stockton & Darlington and the Tees Conservancy, Parliament decided that it was in the public interest to end the uncertainty so, under the Cleveland Railway Act 1861, the company was empowered to complete the railway from Normanby Jetty, on the Tees, right through to Loftus.

Because work was well advanced before the line had become 'public', it took only until 23rd November 1861 to open the section from Normanby Jetty to Skelton near Guisborough. It crossed over the Stockton & Darlington near Cargo Fleet and also outside Guisborough but at neither point did it make any physical connection initially.

The Cleveland Railway was extended to Boosbeck in 1862, and to Brotton in 1865. Skinningrove was reached in 1866 but the final link into Loftus had to

A feature of Saltburn Station was the track and platform extending to the entrance of the railway owned Zetland Hotel. No. 69872 runs round its train on 13 July 1957. *(J.C.W. Halliday)*

await completion of Kilton Viaduct. This consisted of iron girders supported by twelve stone piers which carried the railway at a maximum height of 150 feet above the Kilton Beck.

In order to reach the mines and gasworks in the valley below Skinningrove, a zig-zag line was built. The first leg started north of Skinningrove Station and ran for almost ¾ mile falling at up to 1 in 37 before ending in a reversing neck underneath Kilton Viaduct.

The second leg was much steeper at 1 in 28. This ended in another reversing neck from which trains could proceed along the valley floor to the various sidings. Trains were generally worked with an engine at each end or sometimes with two banking engines at the rear which led the train up the middle leg of the zig zag. They would uncouple from the train prior to banking up the final leg so that they could drop off as soon as the train was under way on the main line.

In 1865, the North Eastern Railway further consolidated its local monopoly by taking over the West Hartlepool Company and with it the Cleveland Railway. It immediately took steps to eliminate the duplication of routes by closing a section of the Cleveland Railway between Guisborough and Flatts Lane. First it built a short connection linking the Cleveland to the former Middlesbrough and Guisborough line at Hutton Junction. This created a through route from Middlesbrough to Loftus but with Guisborough station at the end of a short branch.

The remaining bit of the Cleveland north of Flatts Lane was connected in February 1865 to the Middlesbrough – Redcar line and continued to serve as a goods branch for just over 100 years until October 1966. From 1902 until 1929 a passenger service operated along this line from Middlesbrough to Eston which was reached by a short spur curving off at Flatts Lane.

The foundations of Kilton Viaduct were undermined by ironstone workings and in 1911 traffic had to be suspended for two years. During this period passengers were conveyed by a char-a-banc between Skinningrove and Loftus but freight, including ironstone from Liverton Mines, had to be conveyed to Middlesbrough via Whitby and the Esk Valley line. The viaduct was burried by tipping spoil from various local mines so as to create an embankment across which rail traffic resumed in 1913. The reversing neck of the Skinningrove zig-zag line had to be realigned because previously it had run underneath the viaduct.

The Saltburn Extension

The 1865 Act which merged the Cleveland Railway into the NER also authorised the connecting line between Saltburn and Brotton.

This opened for goods on 1 July 1872 allowing traffic from the mines in the Brotton and Loftus areas to travel direct to the various works on the Tees east of Middlesbrough.

On 1 April 1875, a passenger service was introduced between Saltburn and Loftus serving Brotton and Skinningrove Stations. North Skelton did not open until 1902. Trains leaving Saltburn had to propel back

An ex NER Q6 0-8-0 crossing Upleatham Viaduct between Saltburn and Brotton with a mixed freight in May 1955. *(J. Davenport)*

to the junction before joining the extension line which climbs in a long sweep encircling the town.

Also authorised under the 1865 Act was the Priestcroft Curve between North Skelton and Boosbeck. This opened in 1878 permitting a passenger service to operate from Saltburn to Guisborough. Trains had to reverse into and out of both termini and, in the twentieth century, the service became an obvious candidate for push-pull operation. Most trains also reversed at Brotton and after the First World War there were no regular passenger workings over the Priestcroft Curve.

In 1910 departures for Middlesbrough (weekdays only) for the Guisborough line were at:

6.20 am to	Loftus
8.40	Loftus
9.42	Saltburn via Priestcroft Loop
11.57	Saltburn via Priestcroft Loop
12.51 pm	Guisborough
2.47	Saltburn via Brotton
4.52	Saltburn via Brotton
5.17	Guisborough
6.00	Guisborough
8.20	Guisborough with connection to Saltburn via Brotton
10.48	Guisborough (Wed and Sat only)

The Whitby, Redcar & Middlesbrough Union Railway

The long business of completing the coastal railway between Whitby and Loftus began in July 1866 with the incorporation of the Whitby, Redcar & Middlesbrough Union Railway. Finance for the project was not readily forthcoming and it was not possible to start construction until 1871. Work stopped in 1874 when the contractor went into liquidation. This event was not entirely unforeseen by the railway company which had taken a charge over two of the contractor's locomotives and which it proceeded to sell.

The next task was to find an alternative way of completing the railway and for this the company turned to the NER which took a perpetual lease over the WR & MU in July 1875. The NER employed a contractor of rather more substance who found his predecessor's work, such as it was, to have been unsatisfactory. In particular it was necessary to abandon part of the cliff edge route north of Sandsend because it had collapsed into the sea during the period when work was suspended. Instead Sandsend and Kettleness Tunnels, respectively 1,652 and 308 yards in length, were driven to take the railway through the headlands rather than go round them.

It took until 3rd December 1883 before the 16½ mile route was ready for use.

In addition to the splendid coastal scenery, the railway from Whitby to Loftus was distinguished by the five steel tubular viaducts the principle dimensions of which were:

	Length	Height	Spans
Upgang	330 ft	70 ft	6
Newholm Bank	330 ft	50 ft	11
East Row	528 ft	30 ft	8
Sandsend	268 ft	63 ft	8
Staithes	790 ft	152 ft	17

The first four were all located within the space of 1½ miles. Staithes was by far the longest, highest and the most exposed. Traffic over it was protected by a wind gauge which rang a bell in Staithes signal box when the wind pressure reached 28 lbs per square foot. At that point traffic had to be suspended. If a train was already on its way from Grinkle, it would be stopped at the Staithes outer home signal and if necessary propelled back to Grinkle. The Station Master at Staithes had to send for the nearest platelayer to make an examination of the viaduct.

Class Q6 0-8-0 No. 63389 has just completed the long sweep from North Skelton and is approaching the junction at Brotton. The tracks on the left are from Guisborough.
(J. Davenport)

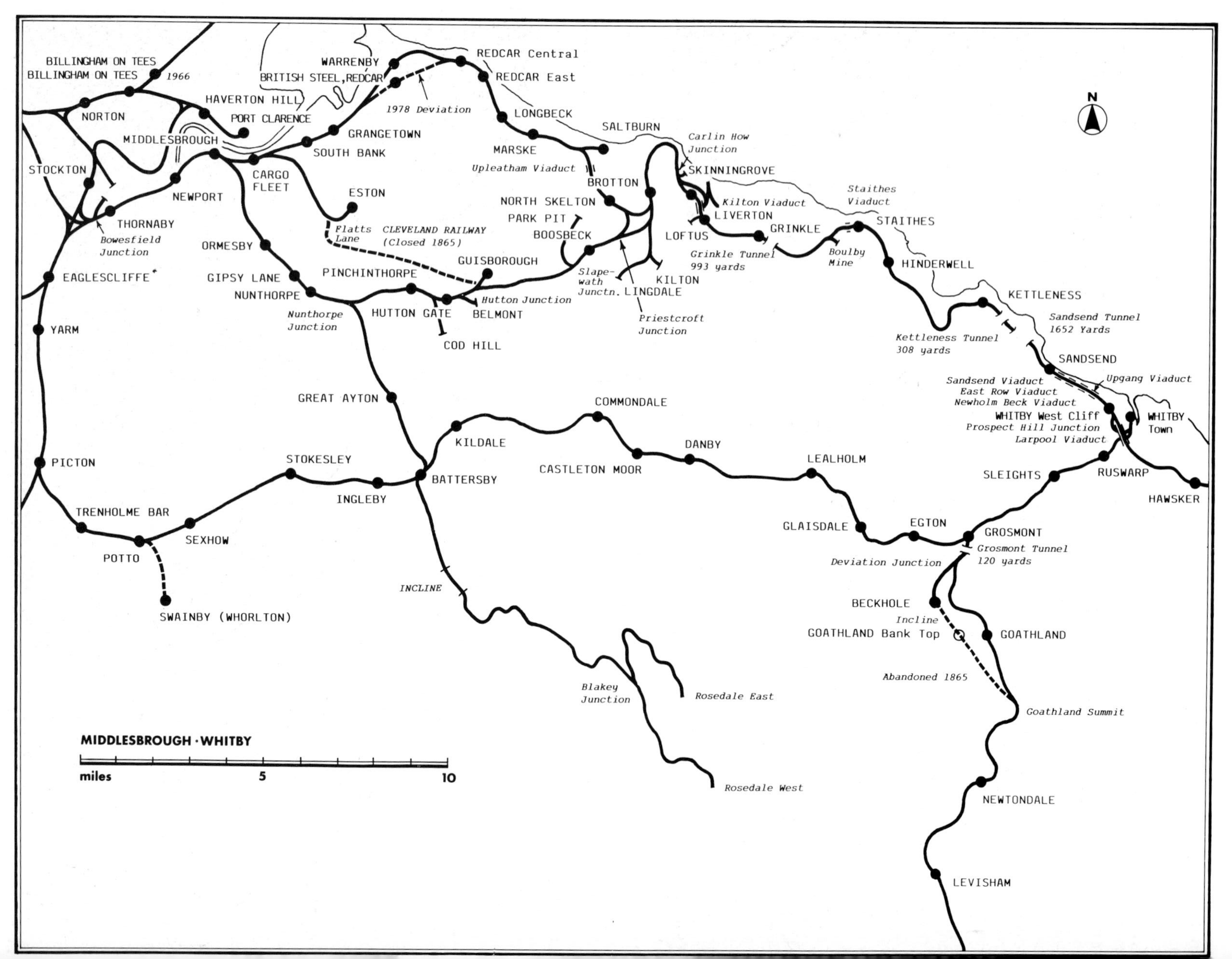
MIDDLESBROUGH · WHITBY
miles
5
10
N
BILLINGHAM ON TEES
BILLINGHAM ON TEES
1966
NORTON
STOCKTON
HAVERTON HILL
PORT CLARENCE
MIDDLESBROUGH
THORNABY
Bowesfield Junction
EAGLESCLIFFE
YARM
NEWPORT
BRITISH STEEL, REDCAR
WARRENBY
GRANGETOWN
SOUTH BANK
CARGO FLEET
1978 Deviation
REDCAR Central
REDCAR East
LONGBECK
MARSKE
SALTBURN
Upleatham Viaduct
ESTON
Flatts Lane
CLEVELAND RAILWAY (Closed 1865)
ORMESBY
GIPSY LANE
NUNTHORPE
Nunthorpe Junction
PINCHINTHORPE
HUTTON GATE
GUISBOROUGH
Hutton Junction
BELMONT
COD HILL
NORTH SKELTON
PARK PIT
BOOSBECK
BROTTON
Slapewath Junctn.
LINGDALE
Priestcroft Junction
KILTON
LOFTUS
Carlin How Junction
SKINNINGROVE
Kilton Viaduct
LIVERTON
Grinkle Tunnel 993 yards
GRINKLE
Boulby Mine
Staithes Viaduct
STAITHES
HINDERWELL
Kettleness Tunnel 308 yards
KETTLENESS
Sandsend Tunnel 1652 Yards
SANDSEND
Sandsend Viaduct
East Row Viaduct
Newholm Beck Viaduct
WHITBY West Cliff
Prospect Hill Junction
Larpool Viaduct
Upgang Viaduct
WHITBY Town
HAWSKER
RUSWARP
SLEIGHTS
GROSMONT
Grosmont Tunnel 120 yards
Deviation Junction
EGTON
GLAISDALE
LEALHOLM
DANBY
CASTLETON MOOR
COMMONDALE
KILDALE
BATTERSBY
GREAT AYTON
INGLEBY
STOKESLEY
SEXHOW
POTTO
TRENHOLME BAR
PICTON
SWAINBY (WHORLTON)
INCLINE
Blakey Junction
Rosedale East
Rosedale West
BECKHOLE
Incline
GOATHLAND Bank Top
Abandoned 1865
GOATHLAND
Goathland Summit
NEWTONDALE
LEVISHAM

'H1' 4-4-4T No. 1330 emerging from the north end of Grinkle Tunnel. The loco dating from 1921 was rebuilt as an A8 4-6-2T in 1934 and survived as BR No. 69889 until 1960. *(D. Ibbotson)*

An Ivatt 2-6-0 heading north over Staithes Viaduct on 13 July 1957. *(J.C.W. Halliday)*

The clouds gather over Staithes Station and Viaduct. The view is to the north in 1958.
(J.C.W. Halliday)

Hinderwell for Runswick Bay from a northbound train on 26 April 1958 just a week before closure. *(J.C.W. Halliday)*

Kettleness looking south in March 1958. *(G.C. Lewthwaite)*

'H1' 4-4-4T No. 1327 emerging from Kettleness Tunnel with a northbound working about 1932. *(D. Ibbotson)*

A8 4-6-2T No. 69881 easing its train into Sandsend on 13 July 1957. *(J.C.W. Halliday)*

Newholm Beck Viaduct, south of Sandsend.
(D.J. Mitchell collection)

V1 2-6-2T No. 67677 on a Middlesbrough to Scarborough train approaching Whitby West Cliff in September 1955.
(J. Davenport)

Whitby West Cliff Station looking south with A8 No. 69881 having piloted D49 No. 62731 'Selkirkshire' on a railtour from Leeds on 23 June 1957.
(G.W. Morrison)

The North Yorkshire & Cleveland Railway

A scene which typifies the Esk Valley Line. The 15.22 Whitby to Middlesbrough near Lealholm on Sunday 2 August 1981. *(G. W. Morrison)*

Popularly known as the Esk Valley Line, the inland route from Teesside to Whitby began as the North Yorkshire & Cleveland Railway. Authorised in 1854, the NY & CR was promoted jointly by the Leeds Northern Railway with which it was to connect at Picton, and the West Hartlepool Harbour & Railway Company. As with most other lines in Cleveland, the main attraction was the prospect of traffic in ironstone. The Leeds Northern was one of the constituent companies which amalgamated on 31 July 1854 to form the North Eastern Railway which took over full control of the NY & CR in 1859.

The line from Picton to Stokesley opened on 3 May 1857 together with the two mile branch from Potto to Swainby which was soon turning out two train loads of ironstone per day. The Swainby branch survived until 1892.

The railway was extended to Ingleby on 1 February 1858 and through Battersby to Kildale on 6 April. Castleton was reached on 1 April 1861 but it took until 2 October 1865 to complete the route to Grosmont on the Whitby and Pickering line. Meanwhile a branch had opened in 1864, initially only for goods, from Battersby to Nunthorpe Junction on the Middlesbrough – Guisborough line. A passenger service between Middlesbrough and Battersby commenced in 1868.

For much of its life, the Esk Valley line enjoyed a modest passenger service beginning with four trains per day in each direction. By 1910 the number had risen to five with departures from Whitby at 7.00 and 10.11 am, 1.30, 3.05 and 5.50 pm. All ran to Stockton via Picton apart from the first train in the morning which reversed at Battersby and continued to Stockton via Middlesbrough but there was a connection via Picton which reached Stockton only eight minutes after the main train.

The Esk Valley line suffered a setback on 23 July 1930 when a stone bridge was demolished by the swollen River Esk in Arncliffe Woods just east of Glaisdale. Traffic was suspended between Glaisdale and Egton until 25 May 1931 when a replacement girder bridge was opened using the old abutments. After only three months use, this too collapsed during floods which swept away one of the abutments leaving the new girder to fall into the river bed. This time a new pier was sunk into the middle of the river and the existing girder was re-erected to reach from there to the bank on one side whilst a similar girder was built to cover the other span. The route reopened for the second time on 27 August 1932 and the bridge has caused no trouble since. In view of the closures which took place on neighbouring lines around 1930 and with an alternative route then available via the

The typical North Yorkshire & Cleveland Station at Ingleby.
(D. Butterfield)

Trains for Whitby (right) and Middlesbrough meet at Battersby on 26 April 1958. The former engine shed on the left disused as such since 1895, stood until 1965.
(J.C.W. Halliday)

Commondale became the first unstaffed station in the Esk Valley in 1954, presumably on account of its remoteness.
(D. Butterfield)

A Middlesbrough to Whitby dmu restarts from Danby in 1966.
(D.J. Mitchell)

Glaisdale Station viewed from a Whitby bound train.
(J.C.W.Halliday)

Egton Station, one of the distinctive NE buildings which still survives albeit now in private ownership. The view is towards Whitby in 1968.
(G.W. Allenby)

coast, the Esk Valley line was fortunate to survive this period.

The 1950 summer timetable shows five departures from Whitby via the Esk Valley at 6.45 am, 12.00 noon, 4.00, 5.50 and 8.30 pm. Only the 6.45 am and 5.50 pm ran to Stockton via Picton with connections at Battersby for Middlesbrough. The other three workings reversed at Battersby to reach Middlesbrough. In the opposite direction, there were three trains from Stockton to Whitby via Picton plus a fourth involving a change at Battersby into one of the two through trains from Middlesbrough. This meant that the Picton to Battersby section had four trains eastbound but only two the other way. The two Sunday trains in each direction ran to and from Middlesbrough via Nunthorpe.

In June 1954, the passenger service was withdrawn west of Battersby and all trains then had to reverse. From May 1958 this operation was rendered a great deal easier with the introduction of diesel multiple units. In the first summer following closure of the coast route these offered up to 15 workings each way between Middlesbrough and Whitby.

A journey along the surviving Esk Valley route is described later. The closed section between Picton and Battersby was double track but from the early 1940s all traffic was worked on the eastbound line west of Ingleby, the other one being given over to wagon storage. At Ingleby westbound trains had to draw forward from the station and then set back across a trailing cross-over before continuing the journey along the 'wrong-line' which was regulated on the staff and ticket system.

From Picton, the branch used to swing south east to Trenholme Bar, a remote station on the Stockton to Thirsk main road. A climb past Black Horse Crossing led to Potto where the platforms were staggered. The principal station was Stokesley where the annual show would bring up to a dozen specials for passengers and quite a few laden with livestock. From Stokesley the line continued to climb towards the Cleveland Hills and Battersby.

Freight traffic ceased west of Stokesley in November 1958 but the line was still used between Picton and Trenholme Bar for wagon storage until 1971. Stokesley closed at the end of July 1965.

The Cleveland Extension Mineral Railway

The building of ironworks at Glaisdale in 1868 prompted the promotion of a 10¼ mile line which would have run across the moors starting at Lingdale Junction, south of Brotton, and joining the Esk Valley route about ¾ mile north west of Glaisdale Station.

The railway was incorporated by an Act of 7 July 1873 and some earthworks were completed before the premature closure of Glaisdale Ironworks in 1876. The railway company tried to press ahead emphasising the potential for mining ironstone in the area through which the line was to have passed. It came to nothing.

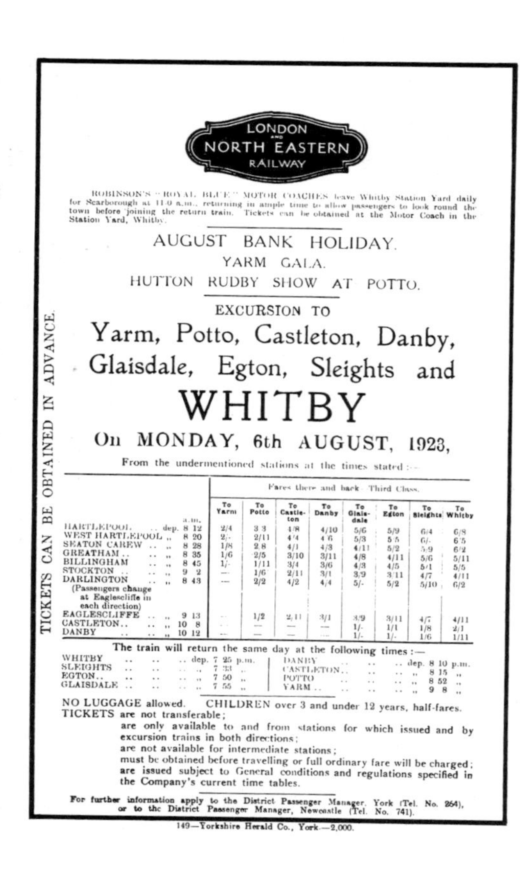

LONDON AND NORTH EASTERN RAILWAY

ROBINSON'S "ROYAL BLUE" MOTOR COACHES leave Whitby Station Yard daily for Scarborough at 11.0 a.m., returning in ample time to allow passengers to look round the town before joining the return train. Tickets can be obtained at the Motor Coach in the Station Yard, Whitby.

AUGUST BANK HOLIDAY.
YARM GALA.
HUTTON RUDBY SHOW AT POTTO.

EXCURSION TO

Yarm, Potto, Castleton, Danby, Glaisdale, Egton, Sleights and

WHITBY

On MONDAY, 6th AUGUST, 1923,

From the undermentioned stations at the times stated :—

		Fares there and back—Third Class.							
	a.m.	To Yarm	To Potto	To Castleton	To Danby	To Glaisdale	To Egton	To Sleights	To Whitby
HARTLEPOOL .. dep.	8 12	2/4	3 3	4/8	4/10	5/6	5/9	6/4	6/8
WEST HARTLEPOOL ,,	8 20	2/-	2/11	4/4	4/6	5/3	5/5	6/-	6/5
SEATON CAREW .. ,,	8 28	1/8	2/8	4/1	4/3	4/11	5/2	5/9	6/2
GREATHAM .. .. ,,	8 35	1/6	2/5	3/10	3/11	4/8	4/11	5/6	5/11
BILLINGHAM .. ,,	8 45	1/-	1/11	3/4	3/6	4/3	4/5	5/1	5/5
STOCKTON .. .. ,,	9 2	—	1/6	2/11	3/1	3/9	3/11	4/7	4/11
DARLINGTON .. ,, (Passengers change at Eaglescliffe in each direction)	8 43	—	2/2	4/2	4/4	5/-	5/2	5/10	6/2
EAGLESCLIFFE .. ,,	9 13	—	1/2	2/11	3/1	3/9	3/11	4/7	4/11
CASTLETON .. .. ,,	10 8	—	—	—	—	1/-	1/1	1/8	2/1
DANBY .. .. ,,	10 12	—	—	—	—	1/-	1/-	1/6	1/11

The train will return the same day at the following times :—

WHITBY .. .. .. dep.	7 25 p.m.	DANBY .. .. .. dep.	8 10 p.m.
SLEIGHTS .. .. .. ,,	7 33 ,,	CASTLETON .. .. .. ,,	8 15 ,,
EGTON .. .. .. ,,	7 50 ,,	POTTO .. .. .. ,,	8 52 ,,
GLAISDALE .. .. .. ,,	7 55 ,,	YARM .. .. .. ,,	9 8 ,,

NO LUGGAGE allowed. CHILDREN over 3 and under 12 years, half-fares.
TICKETS are not transferable;
are only available to and from stations for which issued and by excursion trains in both directions;
are not available for intermediate stations;
must be obtained before travelling or full ordinary fare will be charged;
are issued subject to General conditions and regulations specified in the Company's current time tables.

For further information apply to the District Passenger Manager, York (Tel. No. 264), or to the District Passenger Manager, Newcastle (Tel. No. 741).

TICKETS CAN BE OBTAINED IN ADVANCE.

149—Yorkshire Herald Co., York.—2,000.

The NY & CR joined the Whitby & Pickering at Grosmont where the signal box stood in the angle of the two routes.
(J.C.W. Halliday)

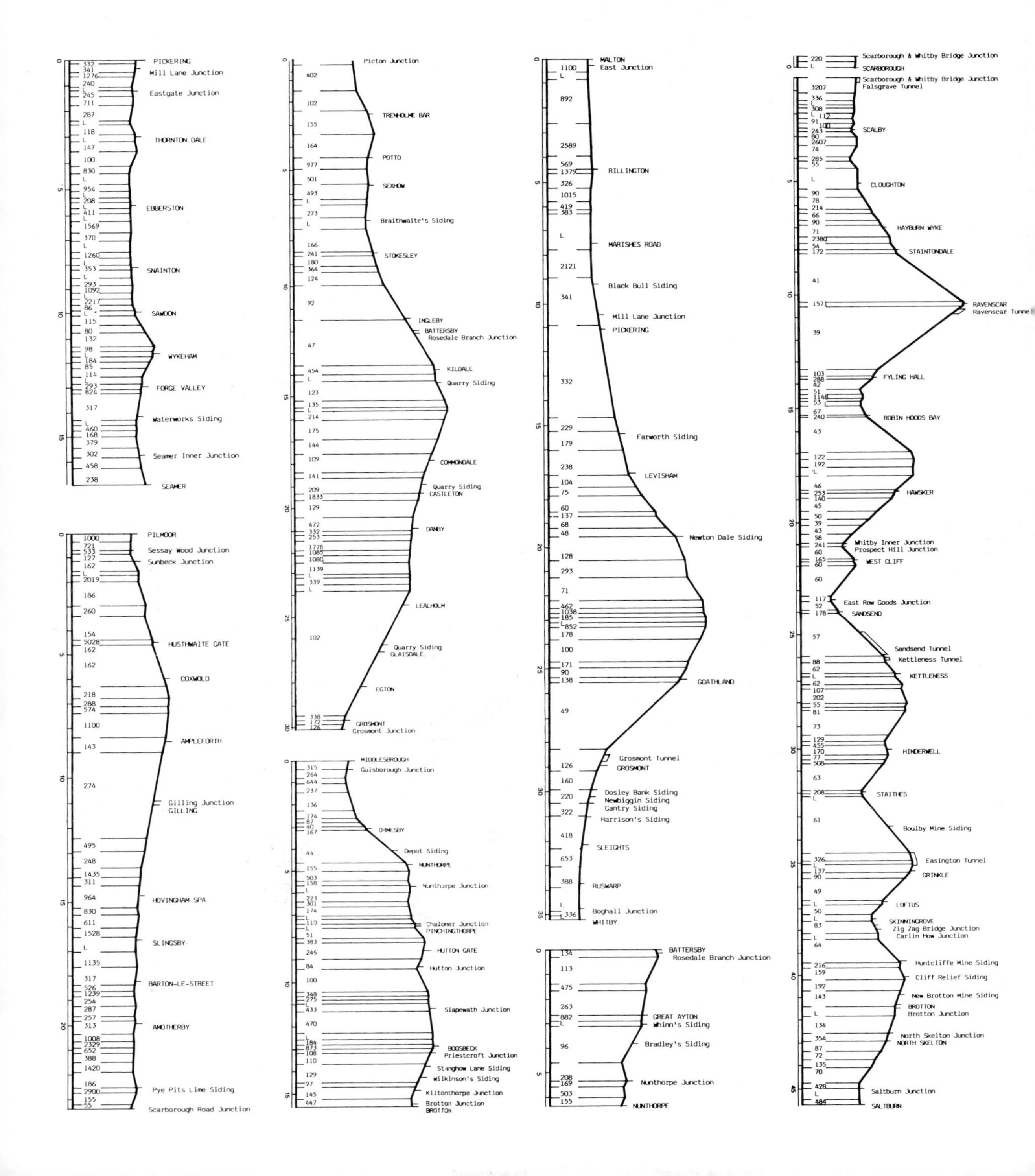

PICKERING
Mill Lane Junction
Eastgate Junction
THORNTON DALE
EBBERSTON
SNAINTON
SAWDON
WYKEHAM
FORGE VALLEY
Waterworks Siding
Seamer Inner Junction
SEAMER
PILMOOR
Sessay Wood Junction
Sunbeck Junction
HUSTHWAITE GATE
COXWOLD
AMPLEFORTH
Gilling Junction
GILLING
HOVINGHAM SPA
SLINGSBY
BARTON-LE-STREET
AMOTHERBY
Pye Pits Lime Siding
Scarborough Road Junction
Picton Junction
TRENHOLME BAR
POTTO
SEXHOW
Braithwaite's Siding
STOKESLEY
INGLEBY
BATTERSBY
Rosedale Branch Junction
KILDALE
Quarry Siding
COMMONDALE
Quarry Siding
CASTLETON
DANBY
LEALHOLM
Quarry Siding
GLAISDALE
EGTON
GROSMONT
Grosmont Junction
MIDDLESBROUGH
Guisborough Junction
ORMESBY
Depot Siding
NUNTHORPE
Nunthorpe Junction
Chaloner Junction
PINCHINGTHORPE
HUTTON GATE
Hutton Junction
Slapewath Junction
BOOSBECK
Priestcroft Junction
Stinghow Lane Siding
Wilkinson's Siding
Kiltonthorpe Junction
Brotton Junction
BROTTON
MALTON
East Junction
RILLINGTON
MARISHES ROAD
Black Bull Siding
Mill Lane Junction
PICKERING
Farworth Siding
LEVISHAM
Newton Dale Siding
GOATHLAND
Grosmont Tunnel
GROSMONT
Dosley Bank Siding
Newbiggin Siding
Gantry Siding
Harrison's Siding
SLEIGHTS
RUSWARP
Boghall Junction
WHITBY
BATTERSBY
Rosedale Branch Junction
GREAT AYTON
Whinn's Siding
Bradley's Siding
Nunthorpe Junction
NUNTHORPE
Scarborough & Whitby Bridge Junction
SCARBOROUGH
Scarborough & Whitby Bridge Junction
Falsgrave Tunnel
SCALBY
CLOUGHTON
HAYBURN WYKE
STAINTONDALE
RAVENSCAR
Ravenscar Tunnel
FYLING HALL
ROBIN HOODS BAY
HAWSKER
Whitby Inner Junction
Prospect Hill Junction
WEST CLIFF
East Row Goods Junction
SANDSEND
Sandsend Tunnel
Kettleness Tunnel
KETTLENESS
HINDERWELL
STAITHES
Boulby Mine Siding
Easington Tunnel
GRINKLE
LOFTUS
SKINNINGROVE
Zig Zag Bridge Junction
Carlin How Junction
Huntcliffe Mine Siding
Cliff Relief Siding
New Brotton Mine Siding
BROTTON
Brotton Junction
North Skelton Junction
NORTH SKELTON
Saltburn Junction
SALTBURN

Rosedale Iron Ore

A view from inside the two road engine shed at Rosedale, built in 1861 and demolished in 1937.
(R. Hayes, courtesy Charles Allenby)

The small village of Rosedale Abbey is today virtually the only sign of permanent life in this isolated valley through which the River Seven flows from its source at Rosedale Head towards Ryedale. In the mid nineteenth century, Rosedale was the source of rich ironstone deposits which caused the North Eastern Railway to construct 19 miles of line to connect both East and West Rosedale with its own system at Battersby.

The 14 mile route from Battersby to West Rosedale was authorised by the North Yorkshire & Cleveland Act of July 1858 and opened on 27 March 1861. Curving sharply away from the NY & CR at Battersby, where there was a small marshalling yard, the branch ran in an almost straight line on a rising gradient until, after 2½ miles it reached the foot of the Ingleby Incline.

1430 yards in length, the incline started at 1 in 11 but the gradient increased to 1 in 5 towards the top. It was double track unlike the rest of the branch, and loaded wagons going downhill, usually three at a time, were counterbalanced by empty ones going up.

From the incline top, the branch followed the 1,000 ft contour employing numerous curves to avoid the adjoining deep, steep sided valleys.

At Blakey Junction, the East Rosedale branch trailed in so that traffic had to reverse direction. 4¾ miles in length, the branch was built by the mine owners at East Rosedale but taken over by the NER which opened it on 18 August 1865. The line headed north to Rosedale Head then required fairly heavy earthworks to curve round and descend to the level of the mine workings.

An engine shed was built at West Rosedale for the opening of the branch. In the early years of the twentieth century, up to five ex Stockton & Darlington 0-6-0s were based at Rosedale hauling ironstone from both termini to the incline top. After 1919 their place was taken by three J24 locos, Nos. 1860, 1893 and 1950. All routine maintenance was carried out at Rosedale Shed. If an engine required to be moved off the branch its centre wheels had to be removed before it could be lowered down the incline.

General goods traffic on the branch was minimal and there was never any passenger service though railway and mining families travelled on the goods trains. The method of working above the incline was staff and ticket with three sections divided at Blakey Junction where there was a man to make sure that the drivers had the correct authority. There were no signals.

The ironstone output reached a peak in 1873. Six years later the mines were closed. They reopened on a number of occasions but never reached the same level of activity. They closed finally in 1926.

The last commercial traffic over the railway was the waste product of the calcining kilns. This was all removed by January 1929 after which demolition commenced. Rosedale Shed closed on 24 January when two of its three engines were transferred to Saltburn. Track and other materials were carried out by rail until the last locomotive (No. 1893) was lowered down the incline on 8 June 1929.

For working traffic onwards from the incline bottom to the blast furnaces on Teesside, a three road engine shed was built at Battersby in 1876. By that time, the ironstone traffic was already past its peak and the shed closed in 1895. It remained standing for a further 70 years during which time it saw various uses mainly storage. During the First World War it housed some restaurant cars but was empty for many years before demolition in 1965.

A Rosedale bound train headed by class J24 No. 1860 at Bloworth Crossing, about 1 mile south of the incline top.
(R. Hayes, courtesy Charles Allenby)

No. 1860 again at Sledge Shoe, one mile beyond Blakey Junction looking towards West Rosedale. *(R. Hayes, courtesy Charles Allenby)*

The Lastingham & Rosedale Light Railway

In 1896 legislation was passed aimed at facilitating the construction of light railways in rural areas. A light railway is not actually defined in the Act. Low speed would be as good an explanation as any because the Act imposed a speed limit of 25 miles per hour in return for relieving some of the obligations on fencing and level crossing protection. Most important the need for a special Act of Parliament for each railway was replaced by a Light Railway Order from the Board of Trade (Later the Department of Transport).

Most light railways promoted around the turn of the century came to nothing. Such a scheme was the Lastingham & Rosedale which would have run from Sinnington to Rosedale Abbey. An agreement was signed with the NER for a junction with the Gilling to Pickering line at Sinnington where the light railway would have had its own station across the road from that of the NER.

Intermediate stations were to have been provided at Appleton-Le-Moors, Lastingham and Hartoft. It was hoped also to have a connection with the NER Rosedale West branch so as to permit the direct movement of goods to the Middlesbrough area. The promoters even ventured to suggest that their line would become part of a through route for passengers between Scarborough and the North. They undertook to operate the light railway with their own locomotives, rolling stock and staff rather than seek a working agreement with the NER believing their method to be 'more economical'.

Their confidence proved to be ill founded. Although some preliminary work was carried out, the scheme fell by the wayside.

The Scarborough & Whitby Railway

The 1865 curve at Rillington and the short lived through service from Scarborough to Whitby may have been an NER response to counter the threat of a direct railway along the coast. If this was the case then the early withdrawal of the NER service may indicate that the company quickly recognised that a coastal line was going to take a considerable time to achieve.

An Act incorporating the Scarborough & Whitby Railway was passed in July 1865. The authorised line would have left the NER west of Scarborough, and rejoined it between Sleights and Ruswarp. The necessary capital could not be raised and the scheme failed.

In 1871 a new Act was granted for a more modest scheme. This was to be an isolated line starting from Gallows Close in Scarborough which was separated by high ground from the NER main line. At Whitby the line was to descend by a 1 in 5½ incline to a terminus on the south side of the Esk.

The necessity of linking up with the NER was recognised in a further Act passed in May 1873 which authorised the connecting tunnel at Scarborough and the substantial Larpool Viaduct which would carry the line to join the proposed Whitby, Redcar & Middlesbrough Union Railway at Prospect Hill. At this stage work at the southern end of the line was progressing but little else then happened during the remainder of the 1870s.

A fresh Act of 1880 revived the earlier powers and this time work did get under way leading eventually to the opening of the railway on 16 July 1885. By an agreement signed the previous year, the line was worked by the NER in return for half the receipts. As was usually the case with such arrangements, there was continued dispute with the owning company accusing the NER of failing to exploit the line fully and the NER responding with complaints about the standards of construction and maintenance of the railway. In 1898 this matter was brought to an end when the NER purchased the Scarborough & Whitby Railway for less than half what it had cost to build.

An exterior view of Scarborough Station about 1910. Parts of the station date from the opening in 1845 though the clock tower was not added until the 1880s. The trams operated between May 1904 and September 1931.
(Peter E. Baughan collection)

Dieselisation in evidence at Scarborough in August 1961.
(P. Sunderland)

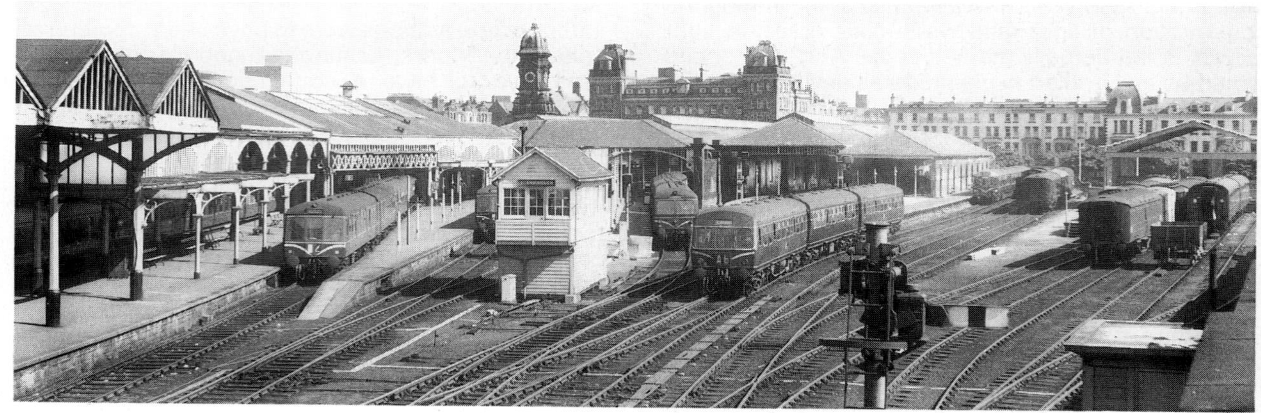

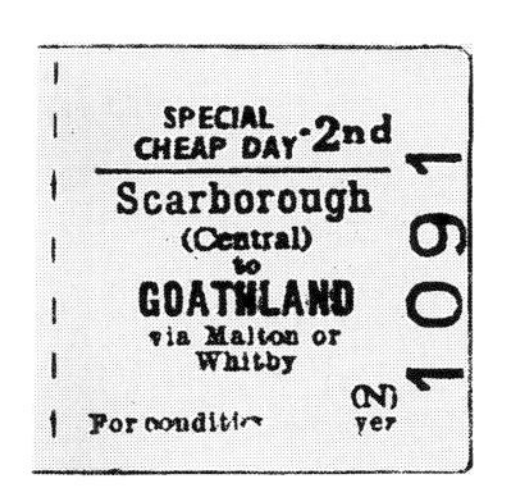

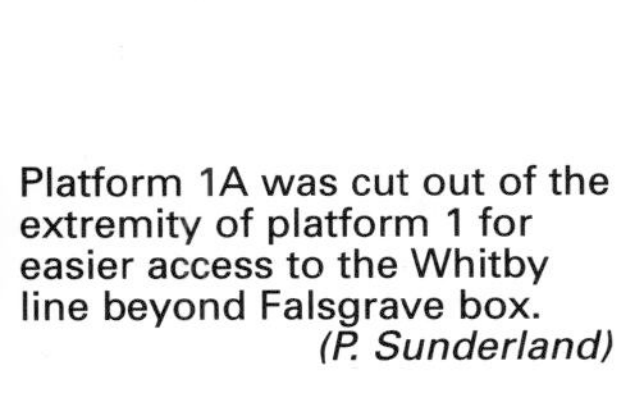

Platform 1A was cut out of the extremity of platform 1 for easier access to the Whitby line beyond Falsgrave box. *(P. Sunderland)*

Errata Volume Two

Two errors crept into the captions to Scarborough line photos in Volume Two. On page 35, 69885 is entering Whitby West Cliff with the 11.40 Scarborough to Middlesborough in August 1957. On page 96, 42085 is at the north end of West Cliff and the signal is clear for the connecting Middlesborough to Scarborough line.

The entrance to Falsgrave Tunnel. *(P. Sunderland)*

Scarborough goods depot was at Gallows Close north of Falsgrave Tunnel. J72 0-6-0T No. 69016 shunts on 4 September 1952.
(John Oxley)

J25 0-6-0 No. 65690 approaching Scarborough with a pick up goods from Whitby on 6 September 1952. The train is on the single line from Whitby. The other track leads to Northstead Carriage Sidings. *(N.E.W. Skinner)*

Dmus passing at Cloughton in the closing months of the Scarborough to Whitby service. The view is towards Scarborough. *(D.J. Mitchell)*

Hayburn Wyke Station looking north at the beginning of the century.
(Peter E. Baughan collection)

A view through a dmu cab passing Hayburn Wyke early in 1965. The station platform was on the other side of the track from opening in 1885 until reconstruction using the same buildings about 1893.
(G.C. Lewthwaite)

A dmu from Scarborough pauses at Stainton Dale before resuming its climb towards Whitby.
(D.J. Mitchell)

The Scarborough & Whitby was a difficult line to work in bad weather. On the morning of 19 January 1959, a combination of mist and sea fret made the rails so greasy that the service was virtually halted all day. There had been no trains on the previous day, a Winter Sunday. The first southbound working on the Monday, the 7.28 am from Middlesbrough was formed of a 3 car dmu. After coming to a stand near Hawsker, it returned to Whitby where the centre trailer was removed but, even with just the two power cars, it fared no better. It was a design fault of the dmus that they had no sanding equipment although on this occasion the steam locos did not do much better.

Class D49 4-4-0 No. 62751 was sent out from Scarborough to assist but could not make any progress with the diesel whose passengers were eventually taken to Scarborough by road arriving mid afternoon instead of 9.58 am.

The next service from Whitby at 11.20 am was worked by 2-6-4T No. 42084 with two coaches. 62751 was attached as pilot at Robin Hood's Bay but the train stalled on the climb to Ravenscar and after running out of sand returned to Whitby.

The first northbound train left Scarborough at 12.52 pm over an hour late with D49 No. 62770 and two coaches. It failed to restart from Stainton Dale and had to leave one coach there. After struggling on to Robin Hood's Bay it again stuck on the 1 in 43 leaving that station. No. 62751 came from Whitby to assist and eventually the two D49s brought their single coach into Whitby at 4.40 pm. They then returned light engine to Scarborough sanding the rails in advance of the six o'clock dmu which was able to follow. Further sanding was carried out by steam locomotives overnight.

The *Whitby Gazette* records an 'unanticipated and unwelcome' delay to an excursion train returning to Scarborough on the evening of Saturday 19 October 1889. 'When the train had nearly reached Peak (Ravenscar), it was found that the engine was not powerful enough to pull the train up the heavy gradient'. The article is rather non-technical but it seems that the train had to be banked up to Ravenscar by the locomotive off the following ordinary passenger train. The excursion then reached Scarborough 'about an hour late' whilst the ordinary train, due at 8.52, did not put in an appearance until 10.10pm.

Above
2-6-2T No. 82029 pilots B1 4-6-0 No. 61049 on a 'scenic' excursion from Huddersfield on 16 August 1959. The train which will have travelled out via Pickering is climbing towards Ravenscar on the return from Whitby.
(N.E.W. Skinner)

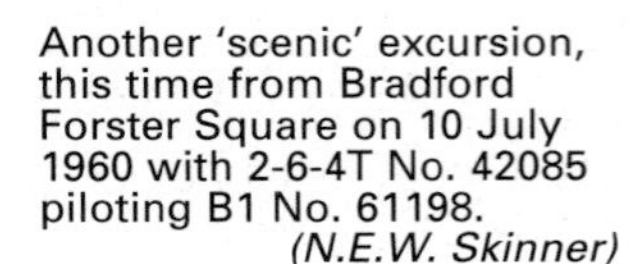
Another 'scenic' excursion, this time from Bradford Forster Square on 10 July 1960 with 2-6-4T No. 42085 piloting B1 No. 61198.
(N.E.W. Skinner)

British Railways were evidently keen to avoid such incidents with the 'scenic excursions' which they ran over the Malton-Whitby-Scarborough lines hence the double heading on the accompanying photographs.

The Special Traffic Notice for Sunday 12 August 1956 shows 'scenic excursions' from Harrogate and Bradford Forster Square running about half an hour apart. The Harrogate train arrives at Whitby Town via Pickering at 12.41, leaves at 3.12 reversing at West Cliff, arrives at Scarborough 4.38 and leaves there at 9.00pm. The Bradford train has a shorter stay at Whitby. It arrives at 1.02pm, leaves at 2.35, reverses at Prospect Hill, reaches Scarborough at 4.04 and departs for home at 8.10pm. Both trains are double headed from Whitby Town to Ravenscar where the assisting engines are detached. They leave Ravenscar at 4.30pm as two light engines coupled together reaching Whitby Town at 5.11pm after reversal at Prospect Hill.

During the final years of the Scarborough and Malton routes, scenic excursions were run by dmus which could offer passengers a much better view. In the peak season of 1959 from 6 July, an excursion ran daily from Scarborough to Whitby, out via Pickering and back by the Coast.

The gradient is apparent as this Scarborough to Middlesbrough dmu pulls into Staintondale early in 1965.
(D. J. Mitchell)

A fine study of an NER slotted post signal at Stainton Dale as 2-6-2T No. 41265 pilots a class B1 4-6-0 on a southbound excursion.
(John Oxley)

The 2.20 pm Scarborough to Whitby approaching Stainton Dale in August 1957 behind 2-6-4T No. 42084. *(M. Mitchell)*

The 'Whitby Moors Rail Tour' pulls away from Stainton Dale on the last day of the Scarborough to Whitby line. *(D.J. Mitchell)*

A southbound train entering Ravenscar prior to the building of the passing loop and second platform in 1908.
(Lens of Sutton)

The 7.10 pm Scarborough to Darlington at Ravenscar on 2 September 1952 behind class B1 4-6-0 No. 61224.
(John Oxley)

Ravenscar Station looking north. Originally named Peak, the station was closed for 12 months from March 1895 because the Scarborough & Whitby Company would not build a house for the NER Station Master.
(G.C. Lewthwaite)

The 10.45 am Middlesbrough to Scarborough climbs towards Ravenscar on 7 August 1957 hauled by Ivatt 2-6-0 No. 43057. *(M. Mitchell)*

The 11.40 Scarborough to Middlesbrough emerges from Ravenscar Tunnel behind class A8 4-6-2T No. 69867 in August 1957. *(M. Mitchell)*

The south portal of Ravenscar Tunnel, 279 yards in length.
(D. Ibbotson)

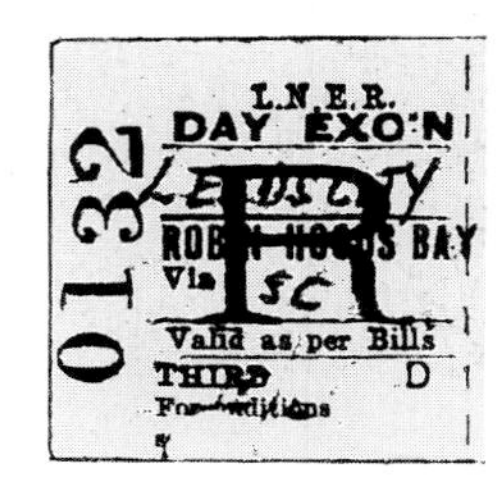

Robin Hood's Bay looking north with a Scarborough dmu entering.
(D.J. Mitchell)

Robin Hood's Bay Station viewed towards Scarborough with the camping coaches in the distance.
(D.J. Mitchell)

The guard gives the signal to restart a Scarborough to Middlesbrough train from Hawsker. *(J.C.W. Halliday)*

The single track from Whitby Town climbed underneath the box at Prospect Hill Junction to join the line in the foreground which had come across Larpool Viaduct. *(G.W. Allenby)*

Class 4 2-6-0 No.43051 has crossed Larpool Viaduct and is approaching Prospect Hill with the 2.57pm express from Scarborough to Middlesbrough, first stop West Cliff then all stations to Brotton then non stop to Middlesbrough. The late running 2.20pm all stations Scarborough to Whitby Town can be seen disappearing down towards Bog Hall having reversed at West Cliff. A bit later, Standard 2-6-4T No.80120 climbs up from Whitby Town with the 4.20pm to Scarborough which it will run round at West Cliff. This was the scene on a Saturday in August 1957. *(A. M. Ross)*

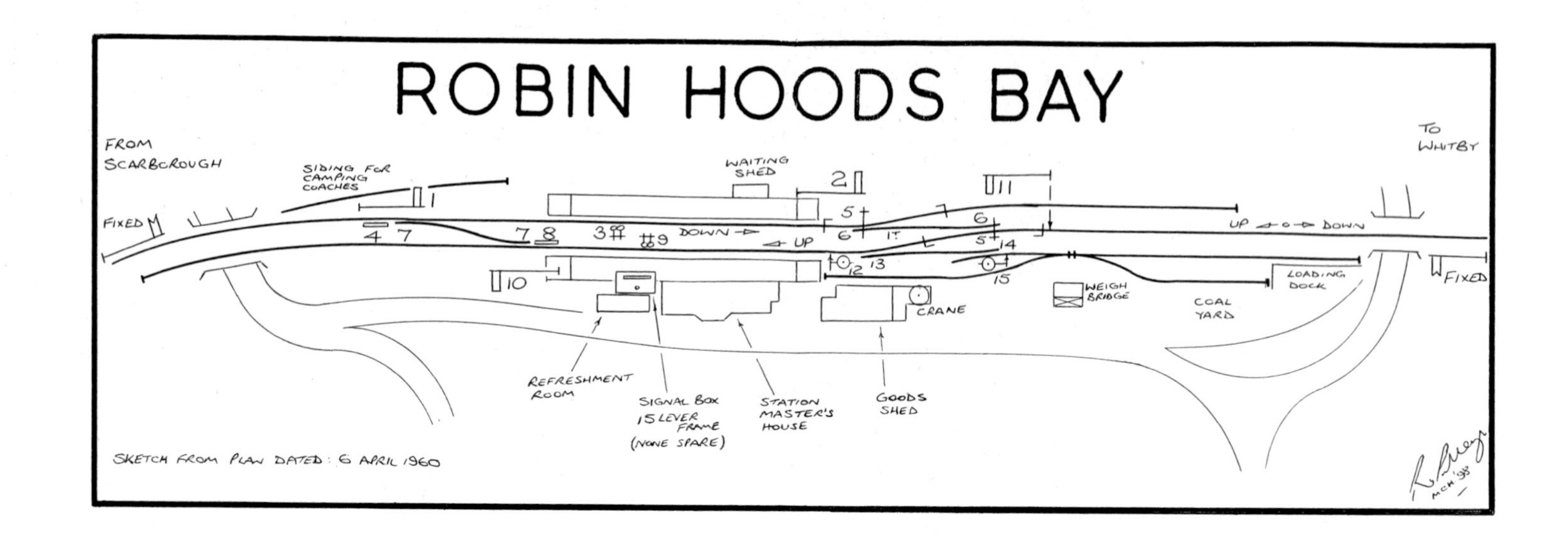
ROBIN HOODS BAY
TO WHITBY
FROM SCARBOROUGH
FIXED
SIDING FOR CAMPING COACHES
WAITING SHED
DOWN
UP
SIGNAL BOX 15 LEVER FRAME (NONE SPARE)
REFRESHMENT ROOM
STATION MASTER'S HOUSE
GOODS SHED
CRANE
WEIGH BRIDGE
COAL YARD
LOADING DOCK
SKETCH FROM PLAN DATED: 6 APRIL 1960

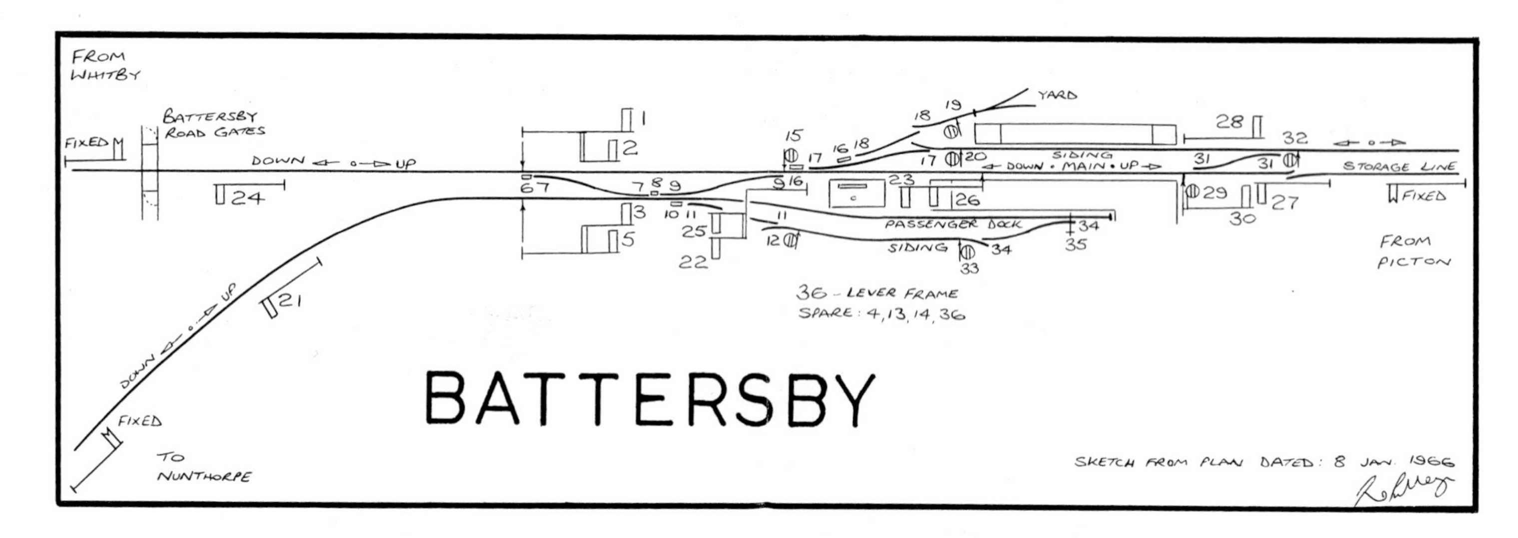
BATTERSBY
FROM WHITBY
FIXED
BATTERSBY ROAD GATES
DOWN
UP
TO NUNTHORPE
YARD
SIDING
DOWN • MAIN • UP
STORAGE LINE
FROM PICTON
PASSENGER DOCK SIDING
36 - LEVER FRAME
SPARE: 4, 13, 14, 36
SKETCH FROM PLAN DATED: 8 JAN. 1966

The Ryedale Lines

t Helmsley the main station building is still there but gone is the glass verandah over the platform. Class 49/1 No. 62730 'Berkshire' calls with the morning York to Pickering train on the last day of regular service, 1 January 1953. *(J. W. Hague, courtesy David Beeken)*

illing Station was the focal point of a small network f lines serving the predominantly agricultural district the angle between the East Coast Main Line and the ork – Scarborough route. The first section to be built vas authorised in 1847 as the Thirsk & Malton Railvay. It was a branch of the York, Newcastle & erwick Railway starting not at Thirsk itself but at ilmoor, six miles to the south. Progress was slow in he difficult years following the end of the 'Railway Mania' but under pressure from the independent Malton & Driffield company, the YN & BR pressed head.

Under the 1847 Act, the T & M would have run irect into Malton by means of a junction with the carborough line just east of the station. Instead, an mending Act of 1852, authorised the T & M to cross ver the Scarborough line and to make its junction vith the Malton & Driffield Railway so as to provide a irect route from the North towards Driffield.

Both the T & M and M & D Railways opened on hursday 19 May 1853 when the ceremonial opening rain left Pilmoor at midday. Pausing at Hovingham to ngage in some mutual congratulation and at lingsby for luncheon, the train reached Driffield at .30. It then returned to Malton where guests were reated to 'a most sumptuous repast'.

The line then settled down to an everyday existence with three passenger trains daily running between Pilmoor and Malton.

The mid 1860s saw an upsurge in the scale of railway promotion which was to lead eventually to the completion of the branch from Gilling to Pickering. The NER was concerned at a threat to its territorial monopoly contained in proposals by the London & North Western Railway for new lines to Teesside and to Scarborough.

In its Yorkshire New Lines Act of 1866, the NER attempted to put an end to speculation by building its own duplicate route from Leeds to Scarborough via Wetherby, Knaresborough, Boroughbridge, Pilmoor and Malton. As mentioned in 'Railways Around Harrogate' (Volume One), only the Cross Gates to Wetherby and Knaresborough to Boroughbridge lines, conceived as part of this plan, were eventually built. In contrast the proposed improvements between Pilmoor and Malton line never came to anything.

South of Pilmoor, a bridge was built across the York to Darlington main line so as to join the Boroughbridge and Malton branches but no track was ever laid. Nor was double track provided between Pilmoor and Malton. Nor was any work carried out on a pro-

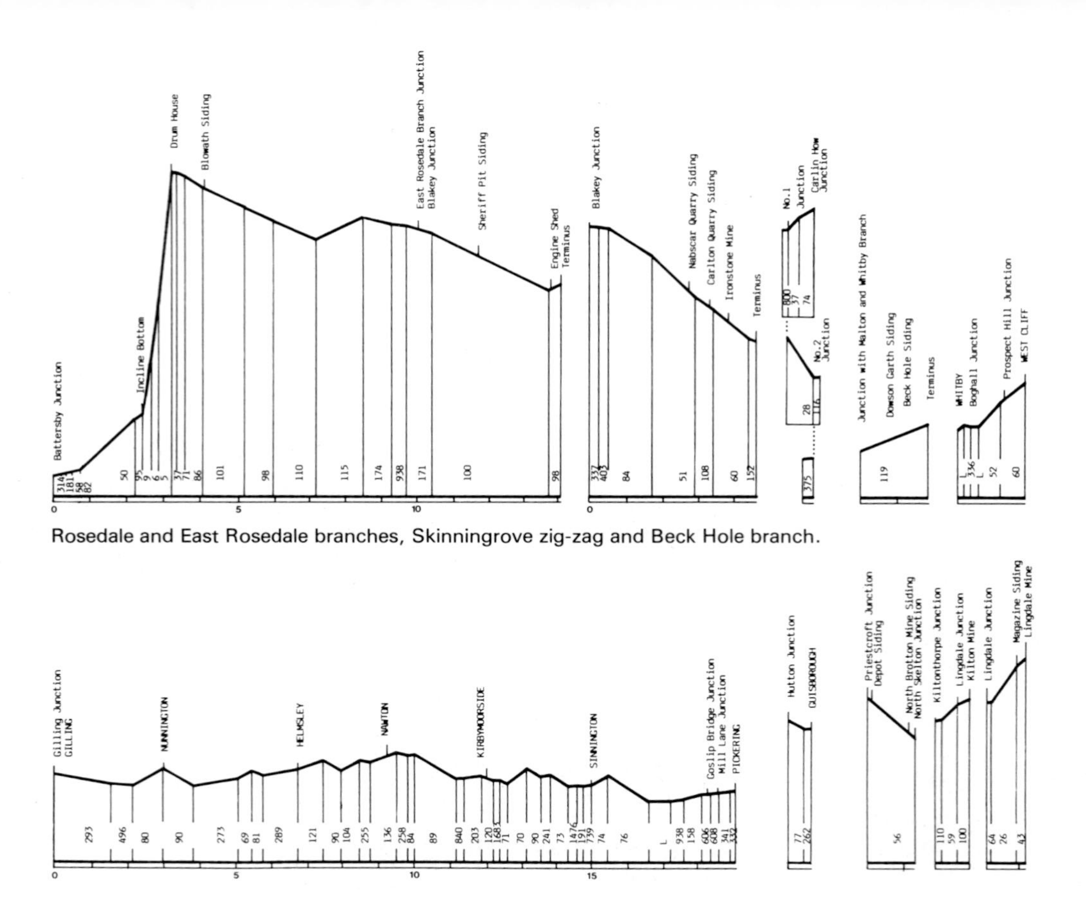

Rosedale and East Rosedale branches, Skinningrove zig-zag and Beck Hole branch.

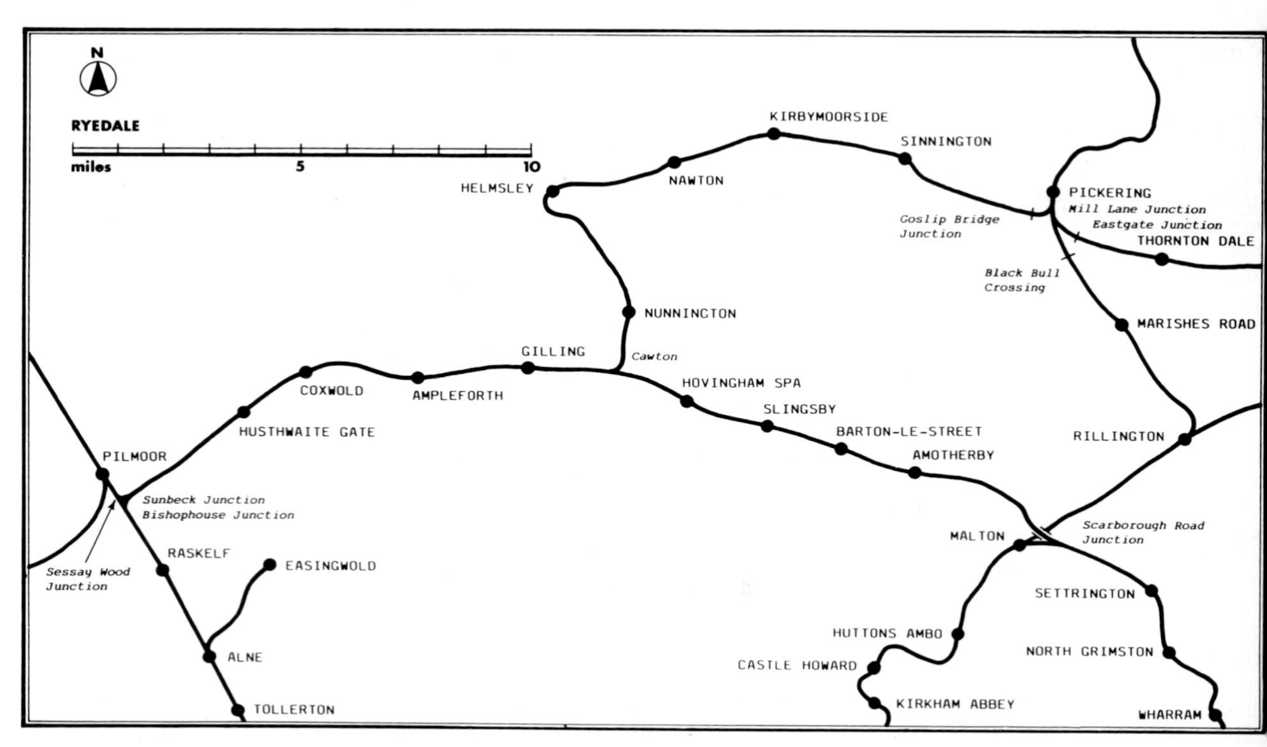

posed 2½ mile 'cut off' north of Malton which would have given direct running towards Scarborough.

The associated scheme for a branch from Gilling to Pickering, also authorised in 1866, proved more fortunate. Again, as recorded in 'Railways Around Harrogate' a number of schemes approved in the mid 1860s had to be abandoned when the trade cycle began to take its downward turn at the end of the decade. The NER contemplated terminating the proposed branch from Gilling at Helmsley. Instead by an Act of 1869, the route into Pickering was altered so as to approach the town from the south and avoid the 400 yard tunnel east of Sinnington which would have been required under the original proposal to join the Whitby line near New Bridge.

The branch was opened in three stages: Helmsley was reached on 9 October 1871, Kirbymoorside on New Years Day 1874 whilst the remaining section to Mill Lane Junction, Pickering opened on 1 April 1875. The curve between Bishophouse and Sunbeck Junctions south of Pilmoor opened on the same day as Helmsley and was eventually to facilitate through running between York and Pickering.

It was the practice of the NER, that where a single track branch joined a double track main line, the branch would itself become double for a short distance so as to form a conventional double track turnout at the junction. Thus both curves from the main line at Pilmoor were double track but at Sunbeck Junction they converged into a single line. The sections from Sunbeck to Coxwold and from Coxwold to Gilling were the first on this route to be converted to electric token working from 15 March 1902.

At Husthwaite Gate, the station house, which is still occupied, was set back from the line on the Pilmoor side of the level crossing. The single platform was at the Gilling side and the points and signals were operated from an elevated ground frame. The first passing loop was at Coxwold, a more substantial

B1 4-6-0 No. 61289 rounds the double track curve from Pilmoor South (Sessay Wood) and is about to enter the single track at Sunbeck Junction. The corresponding curve from Bishophouse Junction was also double. *(J.W. Hague, courtesy David Beeken)*

Sunbeck Junction box seen from a passing brake van in 1957. *(J.C.W. Halliday)*

Sunbeck Level Crossing with its custodians. The board signal indicated the position of the gates. *(M. Mitchell)*

V2 2-6-2 No.60879 west of Husthwaite Gate with the 10.25 Saturdays only Scarborough to Glasgow on 18 August 1962. *(M. Mitchell)*

station with the main buildings on the north side and the signal box on the opposite platform.

Ampleforth Station was a mile and a half from the village at a very remote location. It closed in 1950 but still required to be manned for the level crossing and signals which were controlled from a small hut.

In recognition of Gilling's status as the junction between the Pickering and Malton lines, it was provided with a footbridge in 1894, the only such installation on these lines. In a bid to avoid confusion, Gilling carried the suffix 'For Ampleforth College' since this establishment was nearer to Gilling than it was to Ampleforth Station. From 1895 until the 1920s, a 3ft gauge tramway was employed to carry goods the 1½ miles from the College Siding at Gilling to the school itself. The track ran alongside the mainline for more than half a mile then climbed steeply up the hillside.

The Malton and Pickering routes left Gilling as two single lines. For nearly 1¾ miles, the railway appeared to be double track but there was no junction at Cawton where the two lines simply diverged.

Between Hovingham and the outskirts of Malton, the railway ran parallel to the B1257 road but about half a mile to the north and each of the four stations were on the edge or even some way beyond their respective villages. Barton-le-Street was particularly remote.

The goods yard at Hovingham Spa was enlarged in 1948 to accommodate quarry traffic which was being despatched in up to three train loads per day until 1960 to steelworks on Teesside. Slingsby was a passing loop but with only one platform. Its distinguishing feature was a three storey goods warehouse. Main traffic at Amotherby was the Corn Mill built in 1862 alongside the station.

There were further level crossings and attendant cottages at Swinton, Broughton and Pasture Lane. A quarry siding was opened at Pye Pits near Old Malton in 1856 but disappeared before the Second World War. The River Derwent was crossed by a three arch steel viaduct. Trains from Gilling crossed over the York – Scarborough line to join the Driffield line at Scarborough Road Junction. Here they reversed direction to enter Malton Station by a double track curve.

The route to Pickering parted company with the Malton line at Cawton and immediately turned through 90 degrees. The first station at Nunnington is now a hotel and restaurant. The village of Harome never merited a passenger station but a siding was provided about ¾ mile from the village to facilitate the delivery of coal and the despatch of sugar beet. The small community at Harome Siding comprised four railway cottages housing the crossing keeper and plate layers.

Helmsley Station lay on the tight curve which took the railway from a north westerly to an easterly course. The dominating feature was the glass verandah which protected travellers from the

Standard 4-6-0 No.73163 passing Husthwaite Gate with a Summer Saturday train from Scarborough to the North East in August 1957. *(M. Mitchell)*

Prestige motive power at Gilling. A4 4-6-2 No.60017 'Silver Fox' with the 8.23am Ampleforth College Special to Kings Cross on Easter Monday 1950. *(Chris Wilson)*

A rather more humble G5 0-4-4T No.67273 was in charge of an excursion from Scarborough to York via Pickering on Whit Monday 1950. *(Chris Wilson)*

J27 0-6-0 No.65681 coming off the Gilling line at Bishophouse Junction with a southbound goods on 7 June 1950. The East Coast Main Line was then only three tracks at this point. The up slow line was not laid between Pilmoor and Alne until 1959. *(Chris Wilson)*

J27 No. 65844 heads east through Gilling with a mixed freight in August 1961. *(M. Mitchell)*

elements on the main (Pickering bound) platform. During the First World War a siding was laid from Helmsley goods yard to the Waterloo Plantation some three miles to the west for the extraction of timber.

The largest engineering feature on the branch was Kirkdale Viaduct which crossed the Hodge Beck about a mile beyond Nawton Station. Built of stone, the three arch structure still stands.

Kirbymoorside Station now belongs to the farm machinery firm of Russell's which occupied land adjacent to the railway from the 1920s and was one of its customers. In 1930 a quarry siding was installed on the north side of the line at Spaunton midway between Kirbymoorside and Sinnington just east of Catter Beck level crossing. The siding was last used in February 1948 when a locomotive was derailed on it.

Sinnington Station was a very similar structure to Kirbymoorside but without the passing loop and additional platform. Immediately on leaving Sinnington, the line passed through Riseborough Cutting the largest earthwork on the branch. There were a further four level crossings on the descent from Riseborough at Aislaby Carr, Costa Beck, Westgate Carr and Goslip Bridge. Until 1924 Goslip Bridge Junction marked the end of the single line but on 24 February, the block post there was abolished and the curve was singled round to Mill Lane Junction where the Malton to Whitby line was joined half a mile south of Pickering. This move coincided with the conversion of the block section from Kirbymoorside from staff and ticket to electric token operation.

The passenger service between Malton and Gilling fell victim at the end of 1930 to a policy by which the LNER abandoned certain lightly used trains in favour of its associated bus companies. The four intermediate stations remained open for goods and still booked passengers for the occasional excursion. A similar fate had befallen all the local stations on the main York to Scarborough line the previous September.

A service of four trains per day continued in each direction between York and Pickering. In the 1938 summer timetable there was an additional lunch time working from Pickering to Gilling and back operated by a Sentinel car which came through from Scarborough along the Forge Valley line. In addition there was an unadvertised train from Helmsley in the morning during term time only taking the children to school in Pickering with a corresponding return trip in the afternoon. By 1950 there were just three trains between York and Pickering, one of which later became Saturdays only, plus the school train.

The last day of normal service was Saturday 31 January 1953, a day which is better remembered for the severe flooding in East Anglia and the tragic loss of the 'Princess Victoria' between Stranraer and Larne. The 6.00 pm departure from York was in the care of class D49 No. 62735 'Westmorland'. At Coxwold it passed No. 62730 'Berkshire' on the last up service. Small crowds braved the elements to witness the progress of the train at each station. Arrival at Pickering was punctual at 7.53. After a brief ceremony

The last rush hour at Gilling! Monday 27 July 1964. The six car train on the right headed by the Cravens set is the 8.00 from Helmsley which ran non-stop from Gilling to Scarborough apart from the double reversal at Malton. The seven car train on the left is the 8.39 from Gilling which called at Hovingham, Slingsby, Barton-Le-Street and Amotherby en route for Scarborough. Both trains were Sunday School excursions and were the last passenger workings on the line. *(Charles Allenby)*

A Glasgow to Scarborough holiday train passing Slingsby behind B1 No. 61176 on 29 July 1961. *(D. Butterfield)*

Class B16 No. 61461 accelerates away from Scarborough Road Junction, Malton, and crosses the main line with the 10.25 am Scarborough to Glasgow in July 1961. *(D. Butterfield)*

in which the Pickering Station Master broke a bottle over the engine to declare the line closed, mourners adjourned to the 7.50 Malton train which had been held specially to allow them to get back to York.

Only the Kirbymoorside – Pickering section closed completely. The remainder of the route continued in use for freight and excursions. Gilling even retained a booking office at which Mr Charles Allenby worked between August 1961 and February 1964. The station normally came to life on six days per year when a special train ran to or from Kings Cross carrying pupils for Ampleforth College at the start and end of each term. A second train, in later years a dmu, ran from Leeds.

A couple of days before the end of term, Mr Allenby used to visit the college to affix parcels stamps on to the boys' trunks which were to be loaded into five vans for different destinations which would be delivered to the College Siding at Gilling. The booking office retained a rack of Edmondson card tickets just as at a normal open station. At other times of year, tickets were issued for travel from York usually to customers connected with the College. Tickets could be issued for any journey on BR but in those days there was no national fares manual and the fare had to be obtained from York.

Other passenger movements after 1953 included ramblers excursions, bringing people from the West Riding to stations on the branch. In the other direction there were occasional special trains taking people from Kirbymoorside, Helmsley etc. on, for example, day trips to Scarborough organised by local Sunday Schools. Each summer until 1962, the route between Pilmoor and Malton was used by through trains on Saturdays between the North East and Scarborough. These workings brought prestige motive power through Gilling in the form of 4-6-2 'Pacific' steam locomotives and latterly class 40 diesels. These trains were pulled back from Scarborough Road Junction to Malton Station and vice versa by a loco from Malton Shed whilst the train engine remained at the other end.

Until 5 February 1962, a stone train ran from Thirsk via Gilling and Malton to the quarry at Thornton Dale on the remaining stub of the Forge Valley line. This doubled up as the pick up goods for Coxwold and Husthwaite Gate. After this train ceased, those two stations were served if required by the Malton to Kirbymoorside pick up. This meant that Sunbeck Junction went for weeks on end without seeing a train. By that time the curve from Pilmoor was single track and the one from the south had been lifted. The box boasted three operational levers: a home signal each way plus a direction lever controlling the token-less block from Pilmoor.

The signalman had to open up in case the pick up required to go to Husthwaite Gate which possibly happened once or twice per week. He would then accept the train from Coxwold where the signalman could then issue the token to the driver who would return it after propelling back from Husthwaite Gate to Coxwold. At this time the entire railway between Malton, Kirbymoorside and Pilmoor remained operational albeit normally for the sole use of the goods which did not run every day and not necessarily for the full length of the line. One or two of the remote level crossings had become unmanned though they were attended by platelayers if passenger trains ran. It was at this point that Dr Beeching arrived on the scene to pronounce the end of the entire operation.

An accident on the main line at Pilmoor damaged Sessay Wood Junction in the early hours of 19 March 1963. It was not repaired and the line was cut back to Husthwaite Gate. The last Ampleforth College specials ran on 28 April 1964. A ramblers excursion on 3 May proved to be the last passenger train to Nawton and Kirbymoorside. Then on Monday 27 July two Sunday School excursions, of six and seven coaches respectively, ran from Helmsley and from Gilling to Scarborough. At the end of the following week, on Friday 7 August 1964, the pick up goods made its last trip behind class J27 0-6-0 No. 65894 which was brought in specially. Normally the working had been in the care of a diesel shunter since the closure of Malton shed in April 1963. A contract with the Corn Mill at Amotherby delayed closure of the final section from Malton by just ten weeks until 16 October.

Coxwold looking towards Pilmoor in 1957.
(J.C.W. Halliday)

The 8.40 am (Saturdays only) Scarborough to Glasgow negotiates the crossing at the west end of Coxwold Station behind B1 No. 61274 on 9 August 1958. *(M. Mitchell)*

Scarborough Road Junction on 15 August 1961 with class J27 0-6-0 No. 65844 in charge of a freight from the Gilling Line. The signal box is not the one then in use which was a tall box from which the signalman could see over the Scarborough Road bridge. *(M. Mitchell)*

A J27 0-6-0 ambles through Nunnington station with a modest pay load on 5 August 1958. *(M. Mitchell)*

65844 shunting at Helmsley on 27 August 1959. *(M. Mitchell)*

Latterly the thrice weekly Kirbymoorside pick up was worked by a class 03 diesel. It is seen heading east from Helmsley. *(Charles Allenby)*

The last passenger train to Kirbymoorside, a ramblers excursion from Bradford Forster Square crossing Kirkdale Viaduct on 3 May 1964. *(G.W. Allenby)*

D20 No. 62387 was in charge of a rail tour to Kirbymoorside on 2 June 1957. It is seen running round at what was the end of the branch. *(J. Davenport)*

A train from Pickering entering Nawton Station sometime between 1910 and 1916 behind class 0 0-4-4T No.
088 (later class G5 No. 67317). *(William Hayes)*

he Kirbymoorside to Pickering section closed completely after withdrawal of the passenger service. D49/1
o. 62730 'Berkshire' pauses at Sinnington on the final day in January 1953.
(J. W. Hague, courtesy David Beeken)

The Forge Valley Line

The popular name for this long forgotten byway was that of one of its stations. The railway did not run through the Forge Valley but crossed it in the village of West Ayton. Possibly to avoid confusion with Great Ayton, near Battersby, the station there was known as Forge Valley.

The Forge Valley Railway was actually the official name of a proposed line which reached the stage of an aborted Parliamentary Bill in 1873. This would have run north from West Ayton, through the Forge Valley itself before curving round to join the embryonic Scarborough & Whitby Railway just south of Scalby Station.

When the North Eastern Railway eventually opened the line from Pickering in 1882, it approached Scarborough from Forge Valley Station by going south via Seamer. Here it joined the main line from York just west of its junction with the Bridlington line.

Seamer Station was and still is an island platform. In 1911 a loop was installed on the north side of the layout from Seamer Junction rejoining the mainline at the level crossing end of the station. This line was provided with a platform (No. 1) linked by a footbridge to the island which became platforms 2 and 3. The loop was accessible by trains from Pickering, York or Bridlington which could stand in platform 1 and be overtaken. It was not, however, capable of use by trains from Scarborough to Pickering as might seem logical nowadays. Reversible working only became acceptable in comparatively recent times. Access to the Forge Valley line was by a conventional double track junction. The line then singled a little way along the branch.

At the other end, the Forge Valley joined the Malton to Whitby line at Mill Lane just south of the junction with the line from Gilling. Again the turnout was originally double as far as Eastgate Junction. Later this was abolished and the single track began at Mill Lane. Here trains for both Gilling and Scarborough crossed over onto the 'wrong' line which was reversible for a short distance over the level crossing before the two branches diverged in opposite directions.

Between its two junctions, the Forge Valley line was single track regulated by electric key tokens. There was just one passing place, Snainton. There was a standard design of station building all of which survive in various uses. The gradient was easy with only short stretches steeper than 1 in 100. The line served an agricultural community and enjoyed five trains in each direction in the period before the First World War.

Sentinel railcars were employed from 1928 giving a slightly better frequency of service. The Summer 193[illegible] timetable shows seven journeys each way. There was never a Sunday service on this as on many other North Eastern branches.

Unfortunately the line depended heavily on local traffic. It was hardly a through route and most of the stations were consistently further away from their villages than the parallel road. The last train was push-pulled out of Scarborough by Class G5 No. 67273 at 6.40 pm on Saturday 3 June 1950. This marked complete closure of the line except for the section west of Thornton Dale which was retained for quarry traffic until 1963.

The quarry at Thornton Dale kept open the truncated line from Pickering until 1963. Class G5 0-4-4T No. 67315 trundles through the station on 7 August 1957. *(M. Mitchell)*

NER Class A8 4-6-2T No.
502 passing Snainton with a
rain of empty stock for
carborough in 1936.
(Charles Allenby collection)

The stations of the Forge Valley line were all of a standard design. This is Ebberston viewed towards Seamer. *(D. Butterfield)*

nd this is Sawdon also
ooking towards Seamer. The
ady is standing in front of the
ut which houses the ground
rame. *(Lens of Sutton)*

The Sentinel Railcars

On the North Eastern Railway, an 'autocar' was a push-pull train powered by a 'B T P' 0-4-4 tank engine sometimes sandwiched between two coaches. In early LNER days, this method of operation died out with the demise of the 'B T P' tanks and, surprisingly, there was a lengthy interval before push-pull technology was applied to any alternative engines.

Instead the LNER pinned its faith in steam railcars for more efficient local passenger operation. The first Sentinel car to appear in the North Eastern area was No. 22 which made an experimental run from York to Whitby, out via Pickering, and back via Scarborough on 6 April 1927 with Mr H.G.W. Household as one of the passengers and 'official' photographer.

By the mid thirties, there were 57 Sentinel railcars in the region together with five of the less reliable Clayton steam cars and four diesels. The Sentinels came in two, six and twelve cylinder varieties with the higher powered types being employed on the more steeply graded routes. Nearly all the cars carried names reminiscent of stage coach days. The winter 1935-6 depot allocations included:

Guisborough	2283 'Old Blue'
Malton	2236 'British Queen'
Middlesbrough	2281 'Old John Bull'
	25 'Tyneside Venturer' (diesel)
Scarborough	220 'Defence'
Stockton	2139 'Hark Forward'
	2231 'Swift'
	2232 'Alexander'
	2235 'Britannia'
Whitby	2219 'New Fly'
	246 'Royal Sovereign'
	248 No name

There was, of course, little discernable logic in the LNER numbering sequence before 1946.

The Sentinels had the advantage of raising steam more quickly than a locomotive though they coul lose it just as easily if the crew were not used to them Passengers could enjoy a forward view in on direction only. The engine compartment could ge very hot which was harder on the fireman than th driver who spent half his time driving from the othe end. Access to the bunkers was through doors in th roof which made coaling difficult and ensured that th cars appeared dirty.

The railcars allowed the frequency of service to b improved on some routes. They worked extensiv rosters. 'Old Blue' left Guisborough at 5.14 am fo Middlesbrough and did not finally return unt 9.32 pm. During the day it visited Stockton, Battersb and Loftus. It was handled by a Middlesbrough cre in the early afternoon between the first Guisboroug men finishing and the late turn signing on. On Frida evening and Saturday morning, its place was take by a loco hauled train to allow for a boiler wash out a Middlesbrough Shed. Guisborough was also visite by Sentinels from Stockton and Middlesbroug Sheds and by the diesel 'Tyneside Venturer'. Bot steam and diesel cars worked through from Middles brough to Scarborough in winter but they had insuf ficient capacity for the summer traffic. The railcar could haul an additional coach or van but on th shuttle service between Whitby Town and West Clif two Sentinels were authorised to run together. The had to be facing the same way and both carried a fu crew.

Most of the railcars were taken out of use during th Second World War but the last one survived unt 1948. Their place was in many cases taken by adapt ing class G5 0-4-4 tanks to push-pull working.

In addition to the photographs in this book Sentinel No. 2133 'Cleveland' appears in 'Railway Through Airedale & Wharfedale' whilst No. 2 'Valliant' and diesel railcar No. 232 'Northumbrian feature in 'Railways Around Harrogate Volume One'

A sentinel car entering Grosmont Tunnel en route from Goathland to Whitby about 1932. *(D. Ibbotson)*

esplendent in varnished teak livery, Sentinel car No. 22 reposes at Whitby during a break in its trial run on April 1927. No. 22 was later named 'Brilliant' and repainted green and cream. *(H. G. W. Household)*

horse box was attached for the next stage of the journey to test the hauling capability of the two cylinder 80 orse power railcar. It is seen on arrival at Robin Hood's Bay. *(H. G. W. Household)*

Train Services along the coast

When the WR & MU line first opened, the trains operated between Saltburn and Whitby Town but it was only a year and a half until the Scarborough line came into use. Then some trains ran through from Saltburn to Scarborough leaving Whitby Town Station to be served by a shuttle service to and from West Cliff.

In 1910 there were six trains daily in each direction between Saltburn and Whitby and five between Whitby and Scarborough. Some ran right through with connections to and from Whitby Town whilst others ran from Saltburn to Whitby Town and from Whitby Town to Scarborough connecting with each other at West Cliff. Two of the Saltburn-Whitby workings were advertised as 'autocars' but not any of the trains to Scarborough. There were short workings from Cloughton to Scarborough four times per day.

The Summer 1922 timetable shows six trains virtually at the same times leaving Saltburn but a couple of short workings have appeared between Hinderwell and Whitby Town. There are slightly more trains between Whitby and Scarborough whilst some of the Cloughton trains are extended to and from Stainton Dale. The only Sunday service comprises four return trips from Scarborough to Stainton Dale presumably worked by an 'autocar' but that edition of 'Bradshaw' does not specify.

By the Summer of 1932, the short workings had gone. There were still six departures from Saltburn very similarly timed with seven trains on the Whitby – Scarborough section. On Sundays there were just three trains in the afternoon between Whitby Town and Scarborough.

For the summer of 1933, the northern terminus was changed from Saltburn to Middlesbrough. All trains travelled via Nunthorpe and Guisborough where longer trains were permitted to propel in and out of the station aided by a board proclaiming the word 'seven' at the point where the driver of a 7 coach train should stop his engine. In later summers some trains were routed via Redcar.

There were five through trains between Middlesbrough and Scarborough plus two in the evening between Middlesbrough and Whitby and an additional morning one from Whitby to Scarborough. There were still three Sunday trains but only south of Whitby.

Most departures from Middlesbrough were at 3 or 33 minutes past the hour to fit in with the pattern of Sentinel railcar departures. The combined service to Guisborough was virtually half hourly during the day but with some gaps.

The traffic responded to the changes more than the trains could cope and extras had to be run. In 1934 the service was increased to give nine through trains each way plus the first through Sunday service.

Operation at Scarborough was rendered much easier by the cutting of a bay platform (No. 1A) into the extremity of platform 1. Propelling out of the main part of Scarborough Station to Falsgrave Junction was only permitted with up to two coaches. Longer trains had to depart with the engine at the front and then stand on the main line whilst it ran round before heading off into Falsgrave Tunnel. Traffic on the other routes into Scarborough was also busy and this operation was stretching capacity in the congested station area. From platform 1A, trains of up to five coaches could set off with the engine at the buffer stop end, set back a short distance and then go into forward gear as soon as clear of the points at Falsgrave Junction. The arriving trains could propel into platform 1A. The only snag was that passengers had to walk the length of platform 1 to reach the Whitby train which used to wait three minutes after the advertised departure time to give everybody a chance to catch it. This time it would then make good by the easier manoeuvre compared with departing on time from one of the other platforms.

Further increases in the numbers of trains were made in the following summers. Consideration was given to providing Fyling Hall and Hawsker Stations with second platforms so that two passenger trains could cross there. A passenger train, even one advertised non stop, was not allowed to stand at a passing station if there was no platform. Stations with loops but no second platform could only pass a passenger and a freight or two freight trains. These alterations might have taken place if the Second World War had not put a stop to this passenger boom.

As a guide to the frequency of trains over the coast route, a list of departures from the two Whitby Stations is given for the peak Summer of 1938. There were of course additional excursion and relief trains. It was a problem that the Summer timetable lasted only ten weeks and the railway had to operate way below capacity for most of the other 42 weeks in the year.

After the war, intensive peak services were gradually restored. In 1950 there were 14 trains on a Summer Saturday from Middlesbrough mostly going through to Scarborough. The 8.28 am (SO) stopped only at Kettleness, West Cliff and Stainton Dale and took 2 hours 27 minutes for the 58 miles. Stopping trains took around three hours. Some trains left Middlesbrough via Redcar. The Monday to Friday service was less frequent. There were six trains from Middlesbrough on a Sunday all between 9.15 am and 1.20 pm and returning at half hourly intervals from Scarborough in the evening.

In Winter the service was restricted to three trains each way on weekdays only. Without the shuttle service between the two Whitby Stations only a few Middlesbrough – Scarborough trains had connections to Whitby Town. In 1955 this was partly remedied when operating regulations were relaxed to permit trains of up to two coaches to propel between the Whitby Town, Prospect Hill and West Cliff. Some trains then ran from Middlesbrough to Scarborough via West Cliff and Whitby Town being propelled back to Prospect Hill. Trains starting from Whitby Town for Scarborough could propel all the way to West Cliff at 10 mph then set off for Scarborough without running round.

In 1958 BR blamed the cost of maintaining the viaducts for the decision to close the line between Whitby and Loftus.

With daffodils on the embankment, 2-6-4T No.80117 heads away from Staithes with the 11.40 Scarborough to Middlesbrough on 18 April 1958. *(A. M. Ross)*

L1 2-6-4T No.67765 coming off Staithes Viaduct and entering the station with the 4.20pm from Middlesbrough to Scarborough on 18 April 1958. *(A. M. Ross)*

Departures from Whitby, July 1938

To Scarborough

	Town	West Cliff
	6.45 am	6.56 am
	—	8.24
	(9.15)	9.31
	(9.54)	10.07
	(10.30)	10.50
	—	11.21
	(11.25)	11.42
	—	12.16 pm
SO	12.30 pm	12.44
	(1.15)	1.28
SO	—	1.54
	(2.08)	2.20
	(3.05)	3.24
	(4.10)	4.23
	(6.02)	6.21
	(7.25)	7.51
	(9.38)	10.00
MThSO	10.20	10.36
	Sundays	
	—	10.07 am
	—	10.50
	—	11.21
	—	11.42
	—	12.16 pm
	—	12.53
	—	1.28
	—	1.54
	—	2.19
	—	3.24
	—	4.19
	6.57	7.08
	—	9.58

To Middlesbrough

	Town	West Cliff
	7.14 am	7.22 am
	(9.15)	9.35
	(10.30)	10.49
	(12.30) pm	12.55 pm
	(2.08)	2.32
	(3.05)	3.35
	(5.15)	5.32
	(6.02)	6.20
	—	6.59
	(7.25)	7.49
SO	—	8.27
	—	8.57
	—	9.27
	(9.38)	9.58
SO	(10.20)	10.38
	Sundays	
	—	12.56 pm
	—	3.30
	4.45 pm	5.03
	—	5.23
	—	6.36
	—	6.59
	(6.57)	7.19
	—	7.49
	—	8.18
	—	8.51
	—	9.27
	—	9.56
	—	10.34

To Malton etc

	Town	
	7.07 am	Malton
MFSO	8.00	Malton
	9.20	Goathland
	9.40	Kings Cross
	10.00	Malton
	10.35	Goathland
	11.15	Malton
SO	11.45	Leeds
	12.10 pm	Leeds
SX	12.40	Goathland
SO	12.50	Goathland
	1.32	Malton
	2.15	Goathland
	2.45	Malton
	3.53	Malton
	4.25	Goathland
SO	6.05	Leeds
	7.00	Malton
	9.10	Goathland
	Sundays	
	1.55 pm	Kings Cross
	2.15	Goathland
	4.00	Grosmont
	5.06	Goathland
	6.52	Goathland
	7.35	York
	7.50	Leeds
	8.10	Goathland

Esk Valley

	6.54 am	Middlesbrough (Stockton)
	7.25	Glaisdale
	10.10	Stockton (Middlesbrough)
SO	12.35 pm	Glaisdale
	1.20	Stockton (Middlesbrough)
	3.38	Castleton
	5.47	Stockton (Middlesbrough)
	6.25	Glaisdale
	8.12	Stockton (Middlesbrough)
SX	9.25	Glaisdale
SO	9.25	Middlesbrough
	Sundays	
	6.35 pm	Middlesbrough
	8.36 pm	Middlesbrough
	9.10 pm	Middlesbrough

Connecting trains in brackets
SO Saturdays Only
SX Saturdays Excepted
MThSO Mondays, Thursdays and Saturdays Only
MFSO Mondays, Fridays and Saturdays Only

The coming of the diesels

The demise of the railway, along the coast from Whitby to Loftus was recalled by Stuart Carmichael in the opening chapter. A sad day no doubt but one not entirely without consolation. From the following Monday, 5 May 1958, an enhanced service was introduced on the alternative Esk Valley route between Middlesbrough, Whitby and Scarborough employing diesel multiple units. For the first time all trains served Whitby Town Station.

The new trains were only marginally faster than the old. The dmus were able to make lighter work of the four reversals at Battersby, Whitby Town, West Cliff and Falsgrave but on some journeys the schedules were stretched for example by standing eight minutes at Castleton Moor so as to suit the times of trains coming the other way. Average journey time for the 58½ miles through journey was 2 hours 40 minutes which was about the same as that previously achieved by the steam trains using the coast route if they served both stations in Whitby.

On a route better noted for its scenic qualities than for speed, the diesel trains had the considerable advantage in giving passengers a much improved view including the possibility of travelling immediately behind the driver. Generally this sought after position was first class at one end of the Metro Cammell set and second class at the other.

Another opportunity afforded by the diesels was that of issuing tickets on the train and dispensing with staff at some of the little used wayside stations. This was difficult with non gangwayed coaches. Fyling Hall became unstaffed the day the diesels started.

By 1962 staff had also been withdrawn from Hayburn Wyke, Commondale, Kildale, Great Ayton and Hutton Gate Stations but that was as far as the process got before a much larger bombshell hit the Railways Around Whitby.

The majority of Malton to Whitby trains became dmu operated from 6 April 1959 when both Pickering and Whitby engine sheds closed. The 5.20 am from

DIESEL TRAINS

May 5th will see the inception of the first regular services operated by diesel trains from Scarborough, Whitby and Loftus, and perhaps passengers who have not yet had the pleasure of travelling in this modern manner will appreciate a word or two about the new trains.

Two car units, powered by either two or four 150 h.p. diesel motors will be used to work the new services. Each unit has comfortable moquette upholstered seats for 12 first-class and 105 second-class passengers, the upholstery being predominantly blue for first class and green for second. The interior of the cars is pleasant and restful, with extra wide windows all round which will give passengers a better than ever before view of the magnificent scenery through which the trains travel. Separate non-smoking accommodation is provided. There are toilet facilities and a useful compartment for prams, etc.

FOR SPEED AND COMFORT—

—TRAVEL THE DIESEL WAY

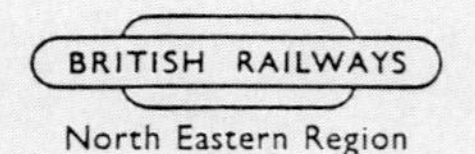

North Eastern Region

McCorquodale & Co. Ltd., London, N.W.1. B6/45.

New Services by Diesel Trains

on weekdays between

SCARBOROUGH — WHITBY —MIDDLESBROUGH and MIDDLESBROUGH—LOFTUS

from 5th May, 1958

SCARBOROUGH—WHITBY—MIDDLESBROUGH

5th May to 7th June, 1958

		Weekdays						S.O.
		a.m.	a.m.	a.m.	p.m.	p.m.	p.m.	p.m.
Scarborough Central	dep.	...	...	11 45	2 50	4 22	8 5	...
				p.m.				
Cloughton		...	...	12 4	3 5	4 37	8 20	...
Hayburn Wyke		...	...	12 8	3 9	4 41	8 24	...
Staintondale		...	...	12 11	3 15	4 44	8 27	...
Ravenscar		...	...	12 18	3 22	4 51	8 34	...
Fyling Hall		...	...	12 25	3 29	4 58	8 41	...
Robin Hood's Bay		...	...	12 29	3 33	5 2	8 45	...
Hawsker		...	...	12 37	3 41	5 10	...	...
Whitby West Cliff	arr.	...	...	12 44	3 48	5 17	8 58	...
	dep.	...	...	12 47	3 51	5 20	9 1	...
Whitby Town ...	arr.	...	...	12 53	3 57	5 26	9 7	...
	dep.	6 55	11 0	1 0	4 5	5 35	...	9 15
Ruswarp		6 58	11 3	1 3	4 8	5 38	...	9 18
Sleights		7 2	11 7	1 7	4 12	5 46	...	9 22
Grosmont		7 10	11 15	1 15	4 20	5 54	...	9 30
Egton		7 14	11 19	1 19	4 24	5 58	...	9 34
Glaisdale		7 19	11 23	1 23	4 28	6 2	...	9 38
Lealholm		7 24	11 28	1 28	4 33	6 7	...	...
Danby		7 32	11 35	1 35	4 40	6 14	...	...
Castleton		7 38	11 38	1 42	4 43	6 17	...	...
Commondale		7 42	...	1 46	4 47	6 21	...	...
Kildale		7 49	...	1 53	4 54	6 28	...	...
Battersby	arr.	7 53	11 49	1 57	4 58	6 32	...	...
	dep.	8 0	11 53	2 1	5 4	6 36	...	...
Great Ayton		8 6	11 59	2 7	5 10	6 42	...	...
			p.m.					
Nunthorpe		8 14	12 7	2 15	5 18	6 50	...	...
Ormesby		8 18	12 11	2 19	5 22	6 54	...	...
Middlesbrough	arr.	8 24	12 19	2 25	5 30	7 0	...	...

S.O.—Saturdays only.

MIDDLESBROUGH—WHITBY—SCARBOROUGH

5th May to 7th June, 1958

		Weekdays				
		a.m.	a.m.	p.m.	p.m.	p.m.
Middlesbrough	dep.	7 30	10 0	1 0	4 30	6 5
Ormesby		7 36	10 6	1 6	4 36	6 11
Nunthorpe		7 41	10 11	1 11	4 41	6 16
Great Ayton		7 49	10 19	1 19	4 49	6 24
Battersby	arr.	7 54	10 24	1 24	4 54	6 29
	dep.	7 58	10 28	1 28	5 0	6 33
Kildale		8 3	...	...	5 5	6 38
Commondale		8 10	...	...	5 12	6 45
Castleton		8 14	10 40	1 41	5 16	6 49
Danby		8 18	10 43	1 44	5 19	6 52
Lealholm		8 24	10 49	1 50	5 25	6 58
Glaisdale		8 29	10 53	1 54	5 29	7 2
Egton		8 33	10 57	1 58	5 33	7 6
Grosmont		8 37	11 1	2 2	5 37	7 10
Sleights		8 45	11 9	2 10	5 45	7 18
Ruswarp		8 49	11 13	2 14	5 49	7 22
Whitby Town ...	arr.	8 52	11 16	2 17	5 52	7 25
	dep.	8 57	11 20	2 28	6 0	...
Whitby West Cliff	arr.	9 3	11 26	2 34	6 6	...
	dep.	9 6	11 29	2 38	6 9	...
Hawsker		9 14	...	2 46	6 17	...
Robin Hood's Bay		9 20	11 41	2 52	6 23	...
Fyling Hall		9 24	...	2 56	6 27	...
Ravenscar		9 33	11 52	3 5	6 36	...
Staintondale		9 38	11 57	3 15	6 41	...
Hayburn Wyke		9 41	...	3 18	6 44	...
Cloughton		9 44	12 3	3 21	6 47	...
Scarborough Central	arr.	9 58	12 17	3 35	7 1	...

FROM 9th JUNE THE SERVICE WILL BE AUGMENTED AND INCLUDE SUNDAY TRAINS

Malton and the evening departure from Whitby remained steam hauled along with their corresponding return workings because of the volume of mail and parcels. These were the responsibility of Malton Shed until that closed in April 1963. For a year steam locos were provided by York Shed but the workings were taken over by class 40 diesels during 1964.

The 1958 closure had only effected four intermediate stations on the coast between Whitby West Cliff and Loftus. Initially both these places benefitted from the new diesel trains but the Loftus service was cut back to Guisborough in May 1960 and Whitby West Cliff closed just in time for the Summer season in June 1961. After that trains to and from Scarborough reversed at Prospect Hill Junction.

The summer 1962 timetable is reproduced for one direction only between Scarborough, Whitby and Middlesbrough, Guisborough and Middlesbrough and between Whitby, Malton and York. All the trains were diesel multiple units except on the Whitby to York service where there was a mixture of steam and diesel. At that time, the North Eastern Region timetable identified dmu services as this was considered a selling point. There were additional excursion trains over and above the timetabled service.

While there were gaps in the Whitby to York service, passengers sometimes had the option of going via Scarborough. Between 21 July and 1 September 1962 there was a connection off the 7.54 pm Whitby to Scarborough arriving York at 10.12 pm. It was also possible to leave Whitby for York on a Sunday at 9.20 am, 12.35 or 4.33 pm changing at Scarborough but the journey took longer than via Pickering and probably involved a higher fare.

In Winter, which lasted from September to June the service was less extensive. There were just five trains between Middlesbrough and Whitby with four going on to Scarborough. Five trains linked Malton and Whitby and there were the morning and lunchtime locals between Whitby and Goathland. There were no Sunday trains outside of the Summer period.

BR publicity for the new diesel trains depicting a scene near Robin Hood's Bay.

Dieselisation in the Esk Valley— A Whitby bound dmu pauses at Sleights. *(Charles Allenby)*

Scarborough to Whitby and Middlesbrough

Summer 1962

Weekdays	a m	a m	a m	a m	SX a m	SO a m	p m	p m	p m	p m	p m	p m	p m	p m	SO p m
SCARBOROUGH CEN				10.23	11.25	11.52	2.05	2.44	4.35	5.04		6.11	7.08	7.55	
CLOUGHTON				10.39	11.46	12.07	2.20	3.00	4.54	5.19		6.27	7.23	8.10	
HAYBURN WYKE				10.43	11.52		2.24	3.04	4.58			6:31	7.27		
STAINTON DALE				10.46	12.00	12.13	2.27	3.07	5.01	5.25		6.34	7.30	8.16	
RAVENSCAR				10.53	12.07	12.20	2.34	3.14	5.08	5.36		6.41	7.37	8.27	
FYLING HALL				11.00	12.14		2.41	3.21	5.15	5.43		6.48		8.34	
ROBIN HOODS BAY				11.08	12.22	12.29	2.45	3.25	5.19	5.47		6.52	7.47	8.38	
HAWSKER				11.16	12.30	12.37	2.53	3.33	5.27			7.00	7.55	8.46	
WHITBY TOWN a				11.31	12.44	12.51	3.07	3.46	5.40	6.06		7.13	8.08	8.59	
WHITBY TOWN d	6.55	9.20	10.30	11.40		12.55		4.03	5.45	6.15	6.50	7.20	8.20		9.15
RUSWARP	6.58	9.23	10.33	11.43		12.58		4.06	5.48	6.18	6.53	7.23	8.23		9.18
SLEIGHTS	7.02	9.27	10.37	11.47		1.02		4.10	5.52	6.22	6.57	7.27	8.27		9.22
GROSMONT	7.10	9.35	10.45	11.55		1.10		4.18	6.00	6.30	7.05	7.35	8.35		9.30
EGTON	7.14	9.39	10.49	11.59		1.14		4.22	6.04	6.34	7.09	7.39	8.39		9.34
GLAISDALE	7.19	9.45	10.55	12.05		1.20		4.26	6.10	6.40	7.15	7.45	8.45		9.38
LEALHOLM	7.24	9.50	11.00	12.10		1.25		4.31	6.15	6.45	7.20	7.50	8.50		
DANBY	7.32	9.57	11.07	12.17		1.32		4.38	6.22	6.52	7.27	7.57	8.57		
CASTLETON MOOR	7.38	10.08	11.18	12.28	Every weekday	1.38		4.41	6.28	7.03	7.30	8.00	9.00		
COMMONDALE	7.42	10.12	11.22	12.32		1.42		4.45	6.32	7.07	7.34	8.04	9.04		
KILDALE	7.49	10.19	11.29	12.39		1.49		4.52	6.39	7.14	7.41	8.11	9.11		
BATTERSBY	7.58	10.27	11.37	12.47		1.57		5.00	6.47	7.22	7.49	8.19	9.19		
GREAT AYTON	8.04	10.33	11.43	12.53		2.03		5.06	6.53	7.28	7.55	8.25	9.25		
NUNTHORPE	8.12	10.41	11.51	1.01		2.11		5.14	7.01	7.36	8.03	8.33	9.33		
ORMESBY	8.16	10.45	11.55	1.05		2.15		5.18	7.05	7.40	8.07	8.37	9.37		
MIDDLESBROUGH	8.22	10.51	12.05	1.11		2.23		5.24	7.11	7.46	8.13	8.43	9.43		

Sundays	a m	a m	p m	p m	p m	p m	p m	p m	p m
SCARBOROUGH CEN		10.33	2.33		5.11	5.45	6.11	7.16	7.39
CLOUGHTON		10.49	2.49		5.30	6.00	6.26	7.31	7.54
HAYBURN WYKE		10.53	2.53			6.04	6.30		7.58
STAINTON DALE		10.56	2.56		5.36	6.07	6.33	7.37	8.01
RAVENSCAR		11.03	3.03		5.43	6.14	6.40	7.44	8.08
FYLING HALL									
ROBIN HOODS BAY		11.12	3.12		5.52	6.23	6.49	7.57	8.17
HAWSKER									
WHITBY TOWN a		11.31	3.31		6.11	6.42	7.08	8.16	8.36
WHITBY TOWN d	10.23	11.40		5.45	6.20	6.50	7.20	8.20	
RUSWARP	10.26	11.43		5.48	6.23	6.53	7.23	8.23	
SLEIGHTS	10.30	11.47		5.52	6.27	6.57	7.27	8.27	
GROSMONT	10.38	11.55		6.00	6.35	7.05	7.35	8.35	
EGTON	10.42	11.59		6.04	6.39	7.09	7.39	8.39	
GLAISDALE	10.55	12.05		6.10	6.45	7.15	7.45	8.45	
LEALHOLM	11.00	12.10		6.15	6.50	7.20	7.50	8.50	
DANBY	11.07	12.17		6.22	6.57	7.27	7.57	8.57	
CASTLETON MOOR	11.18	12.20		6.28	7.00	7.30	8.00	9.00	
COMMONDALE	11.22	12.24		6.32	7.04	7.34	8.04	9.04	
KILDALE	11.29	12.31		6.39	7.11	7.41	8.11	9.11	
BATTERSBY	11.37	12.39		6.47	7.19	7.49	8.19	9.19	
GREAT AYTON	11.43	12.45		6.53	7.25	7.55	8.25	9.25	
NUNTHORPE	11.51	12.53		7.01	7.33	8.03	8.33	9.33	
ORMESBY	11.55	12.59		7.05	7.37	8.07	8.37	9.37	
MIDDLESBROUGH	12.01	1.05		7.14	7.43	8.14	8.43	9.43	

Guisborough Branch

Weekdays only	a m	a m	a m	a m	SX p m	SO p m	p m	SX p m	p m
GUISBOROUGH	7.30	8.12	8.30	9.55	1.30	1.45	4.30	5.42	6.10
HUTTON GATE	7.34	8.16	8.34	9.59	1.34	1.49	4.34	5.46	6.14
NUNTHORPE	7.40	8.22	8.40	10.05	1.40	1.55	4.40	5.52	6.20
ORMESBY	7.44	8.26	8.44	10.09	1.44	1.59	4.44	5.56	6.24
MIDDLESBROUGH	7.50	8.32	8.50	10.15	1.50	2.05	4.50	6.02	6.31

SO Saturdays Only
SX Saturdays Excepted

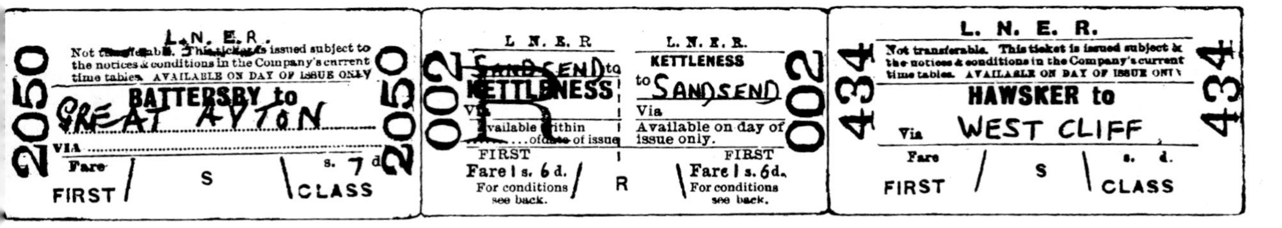

LNER

Whitby Fanciers' Show

Wed. 28th Nov.

RETURN TICKETS

FIRST & THIRD CLASS

at ordinary

SINGLE FARE

(MINIMUM 6d.)

will be issued to Whitby and West Cliff from stations within a radius of 60 miles. Available on day of issue only.

ADDITIONAL TRAINS

		p.m.	p.m.
Saltburn	dep.	7 30	10 36
North Skelton	,,	7 42	10 49
Brotton	,,	7 47	10 54
Skinningrove	,,	7 57	11 5
Loftus	arr.	—	11 9
,,	dep.	8 1	—
Grinkle	,,	8 6	—
Staithes	,,	8 14	—
Hinderwell	,,	8 19	—
Kettleness	,,	8 26	—
Sandsend	,,	8 33	—
West Cliff	arr.	8 39	—

		p.m.
West Cliff	dep.	9 0
Sandsend	,,	9 6
Kettleness	,,	9 14
Hinderwell	,,	9 22
Staithes	,,	9 27
Grinkle	,,	9 36
Loftus	,,	9 40
Skinningrove	,,	9 44
Brotton	,,	9 55
North Skelton	,,	10 0
Saltburn	arr.	10 11

Note—The 8-13 p.m. Loftus to Saltburn will not run on 28th November.

TICKETS CAN BE OBTAINED IN ADVANCE

Tickets, bills and all particulars can be obtained at the stations, also at the usual Town Offices.

For further information apply to the District Passenger Managers at York (Tel. No. 2264), Leeds (Tel. No. 20615) and Newcastle (Tel. No. 741).

FOR CONDITIONS OF ISSUE SEE OTHER SIDE.

YORK, October, 1928.

34302—Ben Johnson & Co., Ltd., Printers, York—4,000

No. 671

LNER

WHITBY REGATTA.

EXCURSION

TO

Staithes, Hinderwell Kettleness

AND

WHITBY (WEST CLIFF)

MONDAY, 23rd AUGUST

		a.m.	3rd Class Return Fares. Staithes.	Hinder-well.	Kettle-ness.	Whitby (West Cliff).
Darlington	dep.	7 53	5/-	5/2	5/8	6/2
Dinsdale	,,	8 3	4/6	4/9	5/2	5/8
Eaglescliffe	,,	8 14	3/11	4/2	4/6	4/11
Cargo Fleet	,,	8 26	3/2	3/5	3/10	4/5
South Bank	,,	8 32	3/1	3/3	3/8	4/4
Grangetown	,,	8 36	2/11	3/1	3/6	4/2
Redcar	,,	8 48	2/4	2/7	2/11	3/7
Saltburn (Passengers change at Marske in each direction)	,,	8 30	1/8	1/11	2/5	3/-
Marske	,,	8 55	1/11	2/2	2/7	3/2
North Skelton	,,	9 10	1/5	1/8	2/-	2/8

The train will return the same day as follows:—

Whitby (West Cliff) dep. 7 40 p.m. | Hinderwell dep. 8 0 p.m.
Kettleness ,, 7 50 ,, | Staithes ,, 8 5 ,,

TICKETS CAN BE OBTAINED IN ADVANCE

NO LUGGAGE ALLOWED. CHILDREN over 3 and under 12 years, half fares.

TICKETS are not transferable and are only available to and from stations for which issued and by excursion trains in both directions; they are not available for intermediate stations and must be obtained before travelling or full ordinary fare will be charged. The Tickets are issued subject to General conditions and regulations specified in the Company's current time tables.

For further information apply to the District Passenger Manager, York (Tel. No. 2264).

YORK August, 1926

868 2050—Petty & Sons (Leeds) Ltd. Whitehall Printeries, Leeds.—2,400

The Sharpening of the Axe

Dieselisation undoubtedly brought a long overdue facelift to the image of the local passenger train—'a complete break from traditional railway practice . . . the sort of thing to bring back business'. (*Trains Illustrated* January 1959) Many services in the North Eastern Region recorded significant increases in patronage.

Unfortunately the substitution of diesel multiple units for steam trains was virtually the only concession to change. In most other respects, the railways continued to operate exactly as before. We now know what scope there was for reducing costs because we have seen it happen on those lines which survived the destruction of the 1960s. We have also seen in recent times how there is scope for the development of rail traffic despite (or even because of) the phenomenal growth of car ownership.

At that time British Railways showed a singular reluctance to shift from a defeatist attitude that operating methods could never be changed and that each stage in the advance of road transport represented a reduction in the role of the railway industry.

Increasing prosperity during the 1950s had been accompanied by growth in personal travel. Although rail traffic had held up reasonably well in absolute terms, as a proportion of a rapidly expanding market, it was in sharp decline. To a growing percentage of an increasingly mobile population, railways were perceived as antiquated, irrelevant to their travel needs and, worse of all, a drain on the taxpayer.

When the railways were nationalised in 1948, it had not been intended that they should be subsidised. Yet after 1952, BR began to incur losses. It was hoped that these would somehow go away and in the meantime they were financed by borrowing, the interest on which created further losses. The programme of piecemeal closures accelerated. Always the choice was between continuing a service exactly as before or stopping it altogether. Economies in operation were not considered.

In 1961, the Government appointed Dr Richard Beeching to take charge of British Railways and to transform it into a viable operation free from subsidy. His brief was to look at the railways in isolation and not to take into account any other social or economic factors.

During 1962, Dr Beeching began to publish a series of incredibly badly drawn maps which purported to show what a small part of the BR network carried the bulk of the traffic. In the summer of that year he announced a moratorium on closure proposals pending the conclusion of his traffic studies. It became obvious that his Report, when published, would contain something far more drastic than had been experienced so far. Nevertheless there was still plenty of complacency in the air right up to the eve of publication in March 1963.

The February 1963 issue of *Modern Railways* predicted that the Report might never be published in full because of the adverse electoral consequences of a programme of major closures. The April edition (which would have gone to press before the Report was published) discussed a suggestion from the Southern Region that stations might become unstaffed as an alternative to closure but concluded that on the whole the idea was impractical. The railway press was evidently more bankrupt even than BR as regards ideas for cheaper methods of operation.

The Beeching Report was duly published at the end of March 1963. It recommended the closure of about half the BR system and promised that these measures, together with a reorganisation of freight traffic to concentrate on goods most suitable to rail movement, would achieve profitability within a period of only a few years. Reduction of costs on loss-making services was not considered, nor was subsidy which Dr Beeching was at pains to stress BR did not want.

When the Report was debated in Parliament in April 1963, the Conservative Government had been in office for 11½ years and would soon be seeking a fourth mandate from the electorate. Surely they would avoid embarking on an unpopular programme particularly one effecting many of their own constituencies. Failing that, surely the opposition would capitalise on the situation by offering an alternative policy. It is a measure of the widespread acceptance of railway closures that the Government pressed ahead and the Opposition did not oppose even though the watered down consultative machinery nicely managed to delay the first impact of closures until the election campaign was in full swing.

The politicians had evidently decided that there was little popular support for the railways. After all the floating voter, who decides the outcome of elections, was at that time typified by the family which had just bought its first second hand car on hire purchase and thought that trains were the last thing which they would ever need.

Even railway supporters were totally convinced (or maybe demoralised into submission) by the Beeching conclusions. The editorial in *The Railway Magazine* for May 1963 began: 'Whether one agrees with all of "the plan" or not it has to be admitted that Dr Beeching's Report is basically correct and backed by such a weight of carefully prepared evidence as to be almost unassailable. It has been described as brutal, brilliant and right'

As far as Whitby was concerned, the Beeching Report could not have been more savage, All three routes—to Malton, Scarborough and Middlesbrough—were recommended for closure along with the surviving branch to Guisborough.

Before this could happen, travellers had to be given the opportunity to object to the Transport Users Consultative Committee. Their task was to assemble evidence of hardship and submit this to the Minister of Transport who would then decide whether closure went ahead. His decision was a political one. Ernest Marples was the Minister who had appointed Dr Beeching and was committed to carrying out his recommendations. The majority of his judgements naturally went in favour of closure. The Guisborough service quickly passed through the procedure and closed at the end of February 1964.

Closure notices were published in respect of all three lines to Whitby early in 1964. The normal procedure at the TUCC public hearings was for those travellers who bothered to speak up to protest that their journeys would not be possible by bus and for BR representatives to say that they would. In the case of seaside lines many of the passengers were tourists who travelled only occasionally and were not necessarily resident in the area. They were even less likely to make any effort to contest closure than the daily commuters on other lines. Hoteliers and traders pleaded for their livelihoods and threatened that Whitby would become a 'ghost town' but they were dismissed as a joke. Rising car ownership would surely make good the loss of railway business in only a few years.

Such was the momentum of railway closures by the summer of 1964, that individual cases barely merited a mention even in the railway press. Those contesting the Whitby closures really must have felt that they were fighting a lone battle.

The outcome was reported in the October 1964 edition of *Modern Railways* in the following brief terms. 'After hearing objections to the NER proposals for closure of all passenger services to Whitby, the local TUCC advised the Minister of Transport that in their view hardship would result from withdrawal but only the Middlesbrough – Whitby line has been reprieved'.

The November issue did enlarge on the matter and conceded that the decision to close the Malton to Whitby service was particularly surprising as the TUCC had reported that 'severe hardship' would result at Pickering and at Goathland.

Looking back it was not merely surprising but incredible that the Government did not make a greater concession to Whitby in the middle of a general election campaign. The Whitby announcement was just one of over 40 given by the Minister on 11 September. The decision to reprieve the Esk Valley route was a short term expedient because the pick up goods happened to run to Whitby that way. Many people had expected the 'main line' to Malton to be the most likely candidate for survival.

Locally the matter became an election issue. The Labour Party had gone into the campaign with no alternative transport policy other than a vague promise to suspend 'major closures' for further investigation. The Labour candidate for the Scarborough and Whitby constituency produced a written undertaking from Harold Wilson that the two condemned Whitby routes were amongst the 'major closures' covered by the manifesto pledge.

By 16 October, Mr Wilson was in Downing Street. Called upon to redeem his pledge, the new Transport Minister, Mr Fraser, explained that due to a technicality in the 1962 Transport Act, he was powerless to reverse his predecessor's decision even though it had not yet been implemented. Apparently not even the Prime Minister had the authority (or the desire) to request that a nationalised industry should slow down on a matter of public concern.

To reinforce the fact that there was to be no change in Government policy, Mr Fraser went on to pronounce judgement in a further 40 outstanding cases ordering closure of all but one.

The December issue of *Modern Railways* reported Mr Fraser's approval of '40 or so' closures without even naming them. It then went on to justify Mr Wilson's broken pledge over Whitby and congratulated the unsung civil servant who had found the 'technicality' in the legislation which had relieved the new Government from having to reverse any closure decisions. Then it devoted almost as many column inches to condemning a threatened increase from 1d to 2d in the charge for using certain station toilets. Not only were closures not opposed they were not even news.

The Conservative MP for Scarborough and Whitby honoured his own pledge by introducing a private members bill under the 'ten minute rule' which is precisely how long it took for that gesture to fizzle out.

It only remained for BR to fix a date for closure of the two routes serving Whitby from the South. On 6 March 1965, ordinary services were supplemented by a 'Whitby Moors Rail Tour' hauled by preserved K4 No. 3442 'The Great Marquess' and K1 No. 62005 which is itself now preserved.

For a couple of years, the North Eastern Region timetable showed replacement buses from Malton and Scarborough to Whitby first with times and then with the more familiar note saying 'bus times not available'. Whitby was listed in the index as a 'place not directly served by rail' with a footnote saying that a rail service was in fact available via Middlesbrough.

Whitby to Malton and York — Summer 1962

Weekdays	**D** am	**D** am	SX am	SO am	SO am	SO am	**D** am	**D** pm	SO pm	**D** pm	SX pm	pm	Sundays pm	Sundays pm
WHITBY TOWN	7.02	7.38	8.48	8.55	9.33	10.22	11.48	12.45	2.00	3.15	5.53	6.56	7.00	7.10
RUSWARP	7.05	7.41	8.53	9.00			11.51	12.48	2.04	3.18		7.01		
SLEIGHTS	7.09	7.45	8.57	9.04			11.55	12.52	2.08	3.22		7.06		7.17
GROSMONT	7.17	7.53	9.06	9.13	9.48	10.36	12.03	1.00	2.17	3.30		7.15		7.26
GOATHLAND	7.26	8.02	9.16	9.23	9.58	10.48	12.12	1.10	2.26	3.39		7.25	7.21	7.37
LEVISHAM	7.41		9.33	9.40		11.05	12.27		2.45	3.54		7.42		7.54
PICKERING	7.53		9.45	9.53	10.26	11.22	12.39		2.58	4.07		7.55	7.52	8.08
MARISHES ROAD	7.59						12.45					8.01		
MALTON	8.10		10.00	10.10	10.43	11.37	12.56		3.13	4.22	7.03	8.15	8.09	8.24
YORK	8.40		10.55*	10.40	11.20	12.07	1.14		3.44	4.51	7.36	8.57*	8.38	8.57

* Change at Malton   SO Saturdays Only   SX Saturdays Excepted   **D** Diesel Train

The Esk Valley in later years

The reprieve granted to the Middlesbrough – Whitby service proved to be more than temporary. In April 1966, the Minister of Transport, by then Mrs Barbara Castle, dropped the first hints towards stabilising the size of the BR network and accepting the principle of subsidy. By that stage it had become clear that despite all the closures, Dr Beeching's promise of a profitable BR was not one step nearer.

The concept of the 'basic railway' was born. As an alternative to closure BR would look at a reduction in the number of staff required to operate the surviving lines. In 1969 all the remaining manned stations in the Esk Valley had their booking offices closed and tickets were issued on the trains.

At that time the Eastern Region had suddenly invented a 'pay train' system whereby only local single tickets could be issued on the trains and that even applied to passengers joining at Middlesbrough and Whitby both of which retained booking offices for the sale of tickets to places beyond the local area. It was not until the 1980s that they settled on the more sensible arrangement of selling all tickets from staffed stations at the booking office leaving the train guard only to deal with passengers joining at stations without this facility. Thanks to his 'Portis' machine and a more comprehensive fares manual, this worthy can now issue a ticket from stations such as Egton or Glaisdale to any point on the BR network.

Other cost saving moves have included the singling of the remaining stretches of double track. Grosmont to Sleights was dealt with in 1972 but it was not until September 1984 that the last three miles into Whitby were rationalised to create what is now just a 'one train section' from Glaisdale. Only one platform at Whitby retains track but there is a siding where a train can be 'locked in' between turns. This move, which involved the closure of Sleights, Ruswarp, Bog Hall and Whitby boxes, followed the demise of the Whitby pick up goods in April 1983. The Middlesbrough to Nunthorpe section was singled in January 1986. The passing loop at Castleton Moor had been eliminated in July 1982.

These cost cutting exercises do not seem to have hit the level of traffic. In 1975, a 33% increase in patronage was recorded. 'A striking example of how passengers can be attracted to branch line services by a vigorous all year round publicity effort'. (*Modern Railways* July 1975).

In May 1976, a slightly improved timetable was introduced giving nine trains each weekday and five on Sundays in Summer and seven weekdays only in Winter. The trains were spaced at roughly two hourly intervals with the Summer extras combining to increase this to hourly out to Whitby in the morning and back again in the late afternoon.

Between Middlesbrough and Nunthorpe there had always been a few rush hour short workings, a hangover from the Guisborough line. The service over this part of the route was stepped up to give an hourly train throughout most of the day and an additional station was opened at Gypsy Lane. In the morning peak there were three departures from Nunthorpe. These had bus connections from Guisborough and through tickets were marketed under the name of 'Easyway'. There were three corresponding return services at 17.10, 17.40 and 18.10 from Middlesbrough.

The 1988/89 timetable shows a slight reduction in the number of trains. From Middlesbrough to Whitby there remain seven each way throughout the year with just one Summer extra – an unbalanced working at 17.45 from Whitby. Four Sunday trains operated from 22 May to 2 October in 1988. In addition, on weekdays there were six trains from Nunthorpe to Middlesbrough but only four in the other direction – some of the peak hour services being balanced by empty stock workings. The bus connections to Guisborough appear to have gone the way of most other attempts at road-rail co-ordination.

Egton retains its station house but out of railway use. A Middlesbrough to Whitby dmu arrives in September 1985. *(David Farrar)*

A Whitby to Middlesbrough dmu restarts from Battersby in 1966. *(D.J. Mitchell)*

A Journey through the Esk Valley

Even if it is starting from Middlesbrough, the Whitby train must now use the main eastbound platform because the bay has been removed. Apart from that, however, the station has been well restored with an impressive stone cleaned facade outside and with the platform canopies and supporting columns repainted in similar blue and white livery to match the class 143 'pacer' units which work most of the services.

Signalling is now controlled by the former Middlesbrough West Box and there is no longer any need for the larger box which used to stand at Guisborough Junction where the Whitby train branches off the Saltburn line. After negotiating level crossings at Cargo Fleet Road and North Ormesby (the first is controlled by closed circuit TV from the gate box at the second) the line enters an area which used to be quite rural. Extensive housing development in the past 25 years has brought extra custom at Marton (formerly Ormesby) Station. This is a wooden structure with just one bare platform. An attempt has been made to tidy up the area previously occupied by the second track and platform by creating flower beds out of old sleepers.

Another product of the 'commuter boom' is Gypsy Lane Station which opened in 1976. This is situated by Marton Lane level crossing, now protected by flashing lights, part way up the 1 in 44 Nunthorpe Bank. When the station was built the track was still double and the disused second platform is now something of an eyesore.

Nunthorpe Station is substantially as it was and here we are reminded of the Stockton & Darlington origin of the route by the B3 number plate on the side of the station house. It was the practice on the S & D to number all buildings with the prefix, in this case B, identifying the particular branch line.

Leaving Nunthorpe the scenery becomes rural and remains so for the rest of the journey. There is another flashing light crossing at Morton Carr before we curve sharply to the right at what was Nunthorpe Junction leaving the disused track bed continuing to Guisborough.

To the left the skyline is dominated by Roseberry Topping, a peak in the Cleveland Hills which rises to 1,051 feet. The railway goes under the Northallerton – Guisborough Road and from that point to Battersby and then along the abandoned route to Ingleby Station, the railway marks the boundary of the North Yorkshire Moors National Park. This is appropriate because this stretch of line really is on the 'frontier' between the Vale of York and the Cleveland Hills with cultivated fields on one side and moorland on the other. Great Ayton Station is about 1¼ miles distant from the picturesque village of that name.

In terms of traffic the reversal at Battersby is a waste of time as few passengers join or alight. Parliamentary powers existed for a triangular junction but the curve leading direct to Whitby was never built. In 1864 the priority was not passengers but ironstone off the Rosedale branch. This used to meet the 'main line' at Battersby where the derelict site to the south of the station was occupied by the engine shed and marshalling sidings. Battersby now serves as a crossing point and the two trains stand side by side in the Middlesbrough bay and in the former eastbound through platform. Only on the rare occasion when a locomotive needs to run round are the tracks used as far as the derelict station buildings and the buffer stops which block off the route to Stokesley and Picton.

Setting off in the other direction, the train soon slows down for yet another crossing protected by flashing lights at Battersby Road. In earlier days it was operated by a crossing keeper and protected by a signal in the form of a rotating red board. Kildale Station is much reduced in size. It used to have two platforms of double the present length. There still remains the footbridge across the station leading to the church.

Kildale is on the River Leven which flows westwards through Great Ayton and then meanders round to join the Tees near Yarm. Leaving Kildale Station, the railway follows the Leven closely for about two miles through rather bleak moorland until it reaches the watershed. Then after passing through a cutting, it encounters Sleddale Beck, a tributory of the River Esk, which flows towards Whitby.

The railway runs alongside Sleddale Beck for two miles then crosses it just before Commondale, a single wooden platform which has been unstaffed since 1954 though somebody has taken the trouble to plant the daffodils which come up each Spring. Traces can be seen of the mile long branch which used to run northwards to a brickworks. There are four bridges over the beck in the next section to Castleton where it flows into the River Esk. The railway passes through woodlands and then takes a sharp curve into Castleton Moor Station which is now reduced to just a single platform. As at other stations on the line, there is a 'welcome to Castleton' poster giving details of local attractions, directions for walkers and a blank space headed 'what's on'. On my last trip over the line, this was the only station where somebody had actually used the space to advertise local accommodation and tea rooms.

The next four stations have buildings in the distinctive style with stepped gable ends which distinguished those on the branch to Pateley Bridge and is also seen at Goathland which was built by the NER in the same period. Danby used to have a passing loop but only for goods trains because there was no second platform. Glaisdale remains the only passing place between Battersby and Whitby but the signals have been removed taking with them much of the character of the country station which had been so well preserved here.

The stretch of line between Glaisdale and Egton is perhaps the most picturesque on the entire route. Passing through a wooded gorge, the train crosses the river three times in quick succession.

There are in total no fewer than 18 bridges across

Tokens being exchanged at Castleton in August 1981 before removal of the passing loop, the second platform and the signal box. *(G.W. Morrison)*

the River Esk between Danby and Ruswarp, nine on either side of Grosmont plus one over the Murk Esk, the tributory which flows in from Beck Hole just before Grosmont Station. As a reminder of the historical origins of our route, since Battersby the mileposts have given the distance from Picton Junction and after Grosmont they are measured from Rillington Junction.

On my most recent journey from Middlesbrough to Whitby we arrived in Grosmont punctually at 14.59. Nobody changed on to the North Yorkshire Moors Railway whose 15.00 departure for Pickering was blowing off at platform 1 more than a minutes walking time away with the level crossing gates open and the signal pulled off. This theme recurs later in the book.

It seems barely conceivable that 100 years ago, the area to the north west of the Esk Valley branch platform was occupied by the blast furnaces of Grosmont Ironworks. There were once a number of sidings off the railway between Grosmont and Sleights serving various bygone industries. Today all is rural as the train negotiates the many curves through the lower Esk Valley. The hills close in towards the river alternately on one side then the other forcing the railway to keep recrossing the Esk.

The girder bridge carrying the main road over the line at Sleights is a replacement for an earlier level crossing. The final bridge over the river is just before Ruswarp Station. Here there is a dam marking the beginning of the tidal estuary and for the rest of the journey small boats can be seen navigating the Esk. The railway takes a sharp curve to the right and Larpool Viaduct comes into view. 120 feet high, with 12 brick arches, this would have been our route in about quarter of an hour were we still permitted to go to Scarborough.

Trains from both Loftus and Scarborough directions used to climb down the embankment on our left passing under the penultimate arch of the viaduct until they reached our level at Bog Hall Junction. The box there has now vanished and the railway scene on arrival in Whitby is rather a sad one. The former goods sidings alongside the river are now used as a car park. On the other side the engine shed is now a ship chandler's store. The station lost its overall roof in 1953. Track was removed from platform 3 some time ago but it had been impossible to stable modern carriages in both platforms 3 and 4 at the same time due to the radius of the curve. With the alterations in 1984, track has vanished from all except platform 1 which is furthest from the station entrance.

The ticket office booked its last passenger on 10 September 1988 and 'red star' parcels ceased to be accepted from the same date. About the only facility left at Whitby is the ability of the driver to replenish the water supply in the train toilets. BR plans a commercial development of the site with railway operation banished from the main part of the station rather like at Saltburn.

The depth to which Whitby Station had sunk by June 1987. 143008 departs from the one remaining tracked platform as the 17.40 to Middlesbrough. *(John Bateman)*

A rare visitor to Whitby, 'Deltic' No.55002 'The King's Own Yorkshire Light Infantry' passing Bog Hall Junction with a return excursion in August 1981. *(G. W. Morrison)*

1989-1998

The previous four pages have been reprinted without amendment from the 1989 edition.

Closure of Battersby and Glaisdale signal boxes took place in August 1989. The simplified layout at Battersby is worked from Nunthorpe box. The driver helps himself to the single line key tokens.

In October 1990, the number of trains between Middlesbrough and Whitby was reduced to four each way on weekdays plus Summer Sundays giving the town its worst rail service since the arrival of the first steam train in 1847. The remaining service was timed around the school traffic. BR claimed that most passenger business was retained by the less frequent trains.

The Esk Valley derived some benefit from improved services at Middlesbrough, developed since 1993 with an hourly 'Trans Pennine' to Manchester Airport and through trains to Newcastle via Durham. The 1998/9 timetable shows the same pattern with four trains to Whitby on weekdays plus two locals from Middlesbrough to Nunthorpe and three the other way. The Summer Sunday service has actually crept up to five through trains each way and operates over a longer period from Easter until the end of September.

Twice during 1997, Whitby was visited by the replica of Captain Cook's 'Endeavour' which brought extra business to the town. The then recently privatised Regional Railways North East responded with additional trains. On the second occasion, from 12 to 15 December, a preserved class 201 'Hastings' unit was deployed.

The main station buildings at Whitby have been cleaned and transformed into a retail development with the one rail track occupying a rather subordinate position. Demolition on the harbour side of the station has exposed to full view the York & North Midland portico, which was previously obscured.

:leveland Potash

the late 1960s, two planning applications were ıade to sink potash mines on the coast of North Yorkıire. In both cases it was promised that output would e moved by rail both on environmental grounds and r sheer practical reasons that this was the best way f transporting it.

One site was at Stainsacre just to the north of awsker. Until 1973, track was left in situ along the sused line from Bog Hall Junction via Prospect Hill ver Larpool Viaduct and as far as Hawsker Station. nfortunately planning objections and a fall in the rice of potash combined to kill the project which ould have guaranteed a heavy freight traffic the ngth of the Esk Valley besides bringing back to life ıe northern most part of the Scarborough line.

Further north at Boulby the story is very different. ere Cleveland Potash despatches up to eight train ads per day. Following closure of the passenger rvice to Loftus in 1960, the railway had been cut back to Skinningrove which continued to be served via Saltburn Junction. The decision to go ahead with Boulby mine led to the rebuilding of four miles of railway through Loftus and Grinkle to a point about one mile short of Staithes. Various bridges which had been demolished were reinstated and the line came back to use in April 1974.

Potash is carried in 93 tonne bogie hoppers either to Tees Dock for export, to Middlesbrough for onward transport by road or direct by rail to Ely and Severnside. In addition rock salt is mined at Boulby and carried out by rail for sale to local authorities for deicing roads. Most trains to and from Boulby are hauled by two class 20 locomotives.

Ventures by passenger trains onto the restored line have been very few. A Branch Line Society railtour on 22 March 1986 was the first public excursion to reach Boulby.

20119 and 20165 in charge of a potash train from Boulby passing Skinningrove on 30 March 1989. *(John Bateman)*

The signal box at Crag Hall, Skinningrove, was closed in February 1970 when the branch from Saltburn was singled. However it reopened on 1 April 1974 with tokenless block from Saltburn Junction and key token working to Boulby. *(John Bateman)*

37079 heads a loaded train of Cleveland Potash round the curve from Brotton towards North Skelton on 20 September 1982.
(Tom Heavyside)

The first public passenger train to reach Boulby, the Branch Line Society Tour on 22 March 1986.
(David Farrar)

assengers to Loftus?

nce the 1980s a number of closed lines have eir passenger trains restored. In most cases the utes had retained, or only recently lost, their ight traffic so the tracks had never been lifted.

There is no shortage of studies being carried t into the possibility of further reopenings, in me cases of lines which have been completely andoned and sold off.

Against this background it seems odd that there s been no suggestion of restoring passenger ains between Saltburn and Loftus.

The combined populations of Skelton, Brotton d Loftus exceed 20,000. There is a half hourly rvice as far as Saltburn (population 9,000). It ould be possible to extend one train per hour as r as Loftus at the cost of one additional dmu. An tra passing loop would be required at Brotton in ldition to the one at Crag Hall in order to retain e freight capacity.

The train would hardly be fast between Loftus d Saltburn. The distance by rail is nine miles cluding reversal at Saltburn West, double that road. But the train would be through to iddlesbrough and Darlington.

Whether the idea is feasible depends on how r the pendulum swings back in favour of rail. ompared with some candidates for reopening, is route has the distinct advantage that it does t require to be reauthorised, repurchased and built. With its gradients, curves and cliff top ews, it would certainly be an interesting journey.

MIDDLESBROUGH – LOFTUS

5th May to 7th June, 1958

	Weekdays							
				S.X.	S.O.			
	a.m.	a.m.	a.m.	p.m.	p.m.	p.m.	p.m.	p.m.
Middlesbrough ... dep.	6 45	9 15	11 15	12 27	12 27	2 27	5 35	8 0
Ormesby	6 51	9 21	11 21	12 33	12 33	2 33	5 41	8 6
Nunthorpe	6 57	9 27	11 27	12 39	12 39	2 39	5 47	8 12
Hutton Gate	7 4	9 34	11 34	12 46	12 46	2 46	5 54	8 19
Guisborough	7 10	9 38	11 38	12 50	12 50	2 50	5 58	8 23
Boosbeck	7 19	9 47	...	...	12 59	2 59	6 7	...
Brotton	7 27	9 54	...	...	1 6	3 6	6 14	...
Loftus ... ... arr.	7 36	10 3	...	...	1 15	3 15	6 23	...

LOFTUS – MIDDLESBROUGH

	Weekdays							
				S.X.	S.O.			
	a.m.	a.m.	a.m.	p.m.	p.m.	p.m.	p.m.	p.m.
Loftus ... ... dep.	7 46	10 18	...	...	1 30	3 30	7 0	...
Brotton	7 57	10 29	...	...	1 41	3 41	7 11	...
Boosbeck	8 4	10 36	...	...	1 48	3 48	7 18	...
Guisborough	8 12	10 44	11 45	1 33	1 56	3 56	7 26	9 16
Hutton Gate	8 16	10 48	11 49	1 37	2 0	4 0	7 30	9 20
Nunthorpe	8 22	10 54	11 55	1 43	2 6	4 6	7 36	9 26
Ormesby	8 26	10 58	11 59	1 47	2 10	4 10	7 40	9 30
			p.m.					
Middlesbrough ... arr.	8 32	11 4	12 5	1 53	2 16	4 16	7 46	9 36

S.O.—Saturdays only. S.X.—Saturdays excepted.

For two years after closure of the coast line, Loftus retained a dmu service to Middlesbrough.

ftus Station photographed from a northbound train on 26 April 1958. The buildings have gone but the ation yard is empty – waiting to serve as a park and ride facility? *(J. C. W. Halliday)*

The North Yorkshire Moors Railway

Heavy diesel power on the NYMR, Deltic No. 55009 'Alycidon' passing Grosmont depot on 9 June 1985.
(G. W. Morrison)

If there were any lingering hopes that the events of 6 March 1965 were other than final, these quickly evaporated. Talk of the Malton to Whitby service being taken over by a private company and/or being subsidised by local councils was at least 20 years ahead of its time. A train did in fact run from Whitby to Goathland in November 1965 when all roads to the village were blocked by snow. Whilst this may have confirmed the value of the railway to those who had opposed closure, it did not bring about the hoped for re-examination of the case and that dmu proved to be the last train over the line operated by British Railways.

By the Summer of 1967, it looked as though track lifting was about to commence but on 3 June a small meeting was held at the home of one of the founders of what was to become the North Yorkshire Moors Railway. At a public meeting at Goathland in October, the NYMR Preservation Society was formed with the object of acquiring at least a part of the Grosmont to Pickering line with a view to operating it primarily as a tourist facility with volunteer staff.

British Railways gave the Society six months to produce a viable scheme during which time track lifting was postponed. In 1968 it was agreed that the Society would buy the line from Grosmont to Goathland Summit signal box together with the land from that point to Pickering. It was envisaged that a terminus to be known as Ellerbeck would be established at the Summit where the Lyke Wake Walk goes across the railway and this would be the limit of the new railway unless and until it were to prove so successful as to allow progressive rebuilding towards Pickering.

At that stage it was believed that acquisition of the track between Ellerbeck and Pickering would be beyond the resources of the Society. In addition it was considered that the proposed 6 ½ mile railway marked the limit of what could be handled by a voluntary society. In the Autumn of 1968, BR gave the Preservation Society permission to work on the line and so began the long haul towards reopening. On February 1969, the first train movement took place when 'Mirvale', a Hudswell Clarke 0-4-0 saddle tank was steamed at Pickering and driven through to Grosmont where the tunnel provided under cover accommodation for the Society's first rolling stock acquisitions.

Society members were able to travel between Grosmont and Goathland on three 'open weekends' during the Summer of 1970 but it was still three years before the railway could reopen to the public. It had been intended that the process of transferring ownership of the railway would follow the pattern established by the Keighley & Worth Valley Railway which had reopened in 1968. This would involve the formation of an operating company in which the

Preservation Society would have a substantial holding.

British Railways would then apply for a light railway order bringing the line within the jurisdiction of the Light Railways Act 1896 followed by a Transfer Order conferring operating powers on the NYMR Company. The use of the light railway order was at that time the only way to transfer ownership of a railway without special legislation.

On 27 March 1971, the functions of both the NYMR Preservation Society and its recently formed operating company were transferred to the North Yorkshire Moors Historical Railway Trust. This body, which is controlled by its membership, has charitable status with resultant tax exemptions including the opportunity for members to covenant subscriptions and donations. The 'Historical' in the title drew attention to the educational part of the Trust's objects. Previously charitable status had been refused to organisations which put railway operation as their main objective. In addition, the Trust was emphasising the historical significance of the Whitby & Pickering Railway in negotiations with the North Riding County Council, its National Park Committee and the English Tourist Board.

These bodies agreed financial support for the NYMR provided that it operated the full 18 miles from Grosmont to Pickering. The County Council purchased the track south of the Summit and leased it to the railway.

The proposed terminus at Ellerbeck never happened. When the NYMR opened to the public on 22 April 1973, it was at 18 miles the longest preserved railway in the Country. There were many, including quite a few people within the NYMR itself, who argued that the Trust had taken on more than it could handle. The scale of the operation, together with its remoteness from centres of population meant that it could not rely solely on volunteer labour. With a sizeable wages bill, the NYMR cannot hope to plough back into the business the same proportion of its income as can be achieved with an all voluntary operation. The railway started off undercapitalised and it was a very slow process for this deficiency to be made good. Inevitably there were some disasters on the way.

In the first summer (the NYMR has so far only operated on a seasonal basis), there were steam trains between Grosmont and Goathland augmented on Saturdays and Sundays only by a dmu running all the way to Pickering. Strictly these trains ran to a point just short of Pickering because of a dispute between the railway, which was backed by the County Council, and the local Council which wanted to see the station demolished and the site redeveloped. Until this was resolved, trains terminated at a temporary platform just north of High Mill level crossing.

1974 saw trains running to Pickering on weekdays during the Summer season but still restricted to the two twin car dmu sets. From 24 May 1975 they were at last able to run into Pickering Station itself.

By way of apologising for the use of diesel power, which at that time had yet to find much support on preserved railways, the NYMR blamed the risk of fire in Newtondale for the decision not to run steam south of Goathland. The truth was that they did not have the steam power with which to do it at the time. 1976 promised a start to regular steam services to Pickering

'Black Five' No. 45428 'Eric Treacy' running round at Grosmont Station. *(John Bateman)*

but the extraordinary hot and dry summer produced a very real fire risk and steam locomotives were banned from the southern section of the line. Since the four dmu cars lacked the capacity for the traffic on offer nor did they have 100% reliability, chaos ensued with some trains being worked at very low speed by a class 08 shunter hired from BR.

The crisis was resolved at the end of the season with the arrival in working order of class 24 No. D5032. This at last gave the NYMR the capability of carrying the numbers of travellers who wished to enjoy the rail journey through Newtondale. It also marked the beginning of a period during which the NYMR became the leader in the field of diesel locomotive preservation. The class 24 was subsequently joined by other BR types including, but not all at the same time, a 31, a Western, Warship and Hymeck, two Deltics and more recently two class 25s.

The diesels gave the NYMR a much needed break. At last there was sufficient power to move long trains the whole way between Pickering and Grosmont. In recent years there has been a shift towards greater reliance on steam power with the gradual building up of an adequate fleet of steam locomotives.

Other developments on the railway have included the building of locomotive works at Grosmont and a carriage shed at Pickering. Colour light signalling has been introduced at Pickering under the control of New Bridge signal box. At Goathland a footbridge has been installed for the benefit of passengers and visitors which crowd this once tranquil wayside station. During 1988 the BR Esk Valley track was realigned at Grosmont to make way for the extension of the NYMR platform and run-round loop to accommodate longer trains.

A Journey on the NYMR

The village of Grosmont lies at the confluence of the Murk Esk with the River Esk and is virtually surrounded by hills. The station has three platforms – two on the 'main line' to Pickering and one curving sharply away on the 'branch' to Middlesbrough. The main buildings are on the former Pickering to Whitby platform and therefore under the control of the NYMR whose trains arrive and depart No. 1 platform on the opposite side.

The level crossing is controlled from a small ground level signal box from which the signalman issues the single line token. In earlier times, the main signal cabin at Grosmont was a very distinctive structure which stood on the junction at the Whitby end of the station. Now it languishes in a corner of the goods yard, now a car park, waiting for a possible new use.

Almost all trains on the NYMR are now steam hauled and are made up of former BR mark 1 coaches of both the 'open' and corridor variety plus some XP64 prototypes.

Leaving Grosmont, the line crosses the river by a stone bridge and then enters the 120 yard tunnel. This dates from 1847 when the railway was adapted for locomotive working. The original tunnel for horse traffic is alongside on the left and is used as a footpath.

The NYMR engine sheds have been built at the south end of the tunnel at what was Deviation Junction. As the locomotive begins to attack the 1 in 49 of the 1865 deviation, the original 1836 route can be clearly seen below on the right making its way to the hamlet of Beckhole. The old trackbed including the incline is a public footpath and many visitors take the train one way and then walk the 'Rail Trail' in the other.

As the hillsides echo to the beat of the locomotive ascending the 1 in 49 towards Goathland, one can only speculate or reminisce of the different classes which might have been at the head of the train were this still a through working from Whitby to York or Leeds.

At the approach to Goathland there is a sand drag protecting the exit from the passing loop as the gradient temporarily eases through the station. Goathland is typical of many NER country stations of the 1860s with the characteristic stepped gable ends as the main feature distinguishing the buildings on the down platform. In bygone days it was a fairly quiet place and it was never thought necessary to provide a footbridge but the crowds who throng the platforms of a preserved railway are a different matter.

Leaving Goathland, the climbing is resumed but at a more modest 1 in 90/100. Just before the summit is reached we can again see the formation of the pre 1865 route as it merges into the present line.

Dominating the skyline are the three domes, often referred to as golf balls, of the Fylingdales early warning station. Goathland Summit is nearly 550 feet above sea level and stands on top of Fen Bog. This rather soggy relic of the ice age was some 20 feet deep at the time the railway was constructed.

Whole trees covered in moss and heather bound in sheep skins were amongst materials sunk into Fen Bog to produce what turned out to be a very durable foundation. The line begins a series of twists and turns through the bracken and heather which provide much colour to the surrounding moorlands as the train enters Newtondale.

There is no road access to the woodlands on the edge of Pickering Forest only footpaths. In 1981 the NYMR opened Newtondale Halt using materials from Warrenby Halt on the Middlesbrough – Saltburn line which was closed when the route was diverted in 1978.

Levisham Station is very remote being reached by a steep twisting minor road from the village which is 1 ½ miles to the east and 300 feet higher up. The station can now be left unattended with the level crossing protected by flashing lights but at busier times it is used as a passing loop.

Between Levisham and Pickering the line runs through extensive woodlands. Two miles of virtually straight track lead to Farworth where the trains occasionally stop to pick up the occupants of some former railway cottages. The line again begins to twist and curve as it negotiates the final length of Newtondale. Then the scenery opens out as the train enters the Vale of Pickering.

New Bridge signal box guards a skew level crossing. It is the only survivor amongst the numerous boxes which used to control the passage of trains through the Pickering area. After the track from Levisham was singled during the First World War, New Bridge marked the resumption of double line working. Today it controls the colour light signals and power operated points in the Pickering Station area.

The final approach to Pickering passes alongside a trout farm. High Mill level crossing, which mainly gives access to the NYMR car park, is protected by flashing lights. The train passes the foot of Pickering Castle and enters the curved platforms.

Prior to 1953, Pickering boasted a typical York & North Midland roof hence the high supporting walls. The main (formerly York bound) platform retains the canopy which was installed to replace the overall roof. Although the platforms are low requiring steps to alight from the train, the adjoining rooms are even lower requiring customers to step down into the shop and buffet. The locomotive draws forward into a head shunt occupying the short distance to what was Bridge Street level crossing where the line has been walled off.

Towards Whitby?

The story of the North Yorkshire Moors Railway has been one of achievement reflecting great credit on the staff and members of the Trust. Much, of course, remains to be done. Station platforms need extending and an additional passing loop is required to split the Goathland to Levisham section if the available traffic is to be accommodated. As on all preserved railways, there is a continual battle to keep pace with the maintenance required by old locomotives, rolling stock and other equipment.

The question now faced by the NYMR is whether it can deal both with these ongoing commitments and with the need to reach Whitby.

Despite its many qualities, the NYMR fails in that it does not really go anywhere. At Pickering the railway almost literally hits a brick wall where there used to be a level crossing leading on to Malton and York. But at least Pickering is a sizeable town, full of tourists and capable of both generating traffic for the railway and of providing facilities for passengers arriving there by train. A reason why the National Park authorities supported reopening to Pickering was that they wanted tourists to be conveyed through the park to a logical destination and not just deposited at Ellerbeck.

It is at the northern end of the line where the problem lies. As the editor of *Moors Line* (Winter 1987/88) so aptly put it, many passengers cannot even pronounce the name of the station where they are 'dumped' 6¼ miles short of the logical destination which would be Whitby. Grosmont has hardly any facilities for tourists arriving there nor is it capable of originating traffic on any scale.

The irony is that there is no brick wall marking the end of the line at Grosmont but a connection into the Esk Valley Line. This is such a tenuous link with the main body of the BR network that one can virtually discount incoming traffic from further afield than the North East. But why cannot NYMR customers travel to and from Whitby? The trains just do not connect, a fact which was recognised in the Summer of 1988 when the NYMR advertised Whitby connections employing a mini bus to negotiate the steep and narrow roads from Grosmont. This is criminal when there is a parallel train service but with departures sometimes fixed literally one minute before the arrival of the other company's train.

The NYMR preferred solution is to run its own trains into Whitby both to tap the extra traffic potential and to avoid 'dumping' passengers with nothing to do at Grosmont. The question is how? Two ideas which have been ventilated in public are non-starters. Let us hope that we would have to wait a very long time for BR to close the Esk Valley line. Nor is it practical to relay a second track because the line has been slewed all over the formation to get a better alignment particularly between Grosmont and Sleights.

The single track between Grosmont and Whitby is anything but fully utilised and NYMR services could be accommodated with various alterations to the track layout and signalling. There is at the moment no precedent for this and the BR position is that all trains would have to be operated by their staff who would have to come from Thornaby and who, in any case, could not be made available on a seasonal basis. It is disgraceful that local authority money has been wasted on a 'feasibility study' just to tell us that the track slewing and the BR staffing options are too expensive.

It would be in keeping with BR policy of seeking to contain subsidies on lines such as the Esk Valley if some of the costs could be shared. Maybe growing talk of 'privatisation' will cause a solution to emerge. Not that the NYMR Trust is unanimous in wanting to press on to Whitby. The arguments for and against seem vaguely reminiscent of the Ellerbeck – Pickering dilemma nearly twenty years ago but we know how that was resolved.

Surely the immediate answer is for BR to exploit its Grosmont to Whitby link by putting on extra trains and marketing jointly a connecting service with the NYMR which could establish its presence in Whitby by reopening the booking office there. This solution would lack the prestige of preserved trains actually steaming into Whitby but would go a long way towards ending the isolation of the NYMR. There are many times of day when a dmu stands in Whitby long enough to do an additional trip to Grosmont and back. Things may not be that simple as the BR driver is probably entitled to his PNB (personal needs break). Such problems would be overcome if Whitby was in a PTE area!

The editorial in *Moorsline* (Winter 1987/88) concluded:

'The Whitby scheme has all the hallmarks of common sense with benefits of magnitude to all parties involved. Have you the faith to travel to Whitby?

The question is not going to go away until a solution is found.

K1 2-6-0 No. 62005 which worked 'The Whitby Moors Rail Tour' in 1965 is preserved on the NYMR. It is seen above Beck Hole attacking the 1 in 49 climb to Goathland on 29 April 1984. *(G.W. Morrison)*

1989 to 1998

Again the previous four pages have been reprinted without amendment. The final comment about the Whitby question not going away has certainly proved accurate. Whether an answer has emerged is maybe a little too early to comment. The spring 1998 edition of *Moors Line* again alluded to the subject and there has been speculation in the national railway press.

Meanwhile much work has been done on the NYMR itself. The layout at Grosmont has been expanded into space at the Whitby end created by slewing the surviving Esk Valley track onto the northern most side of the formation. Platform 2 has been extended whilst platform 3 has been rebuilt into an island with an outer face, now platform 4, on what used to be the back road. New carriage sidings have been laid beyond the station, towards Whitby, and it is hoped that they might eventually gain a roof over them. A 52 lever signal box was commissioned in 1996.

At Pickering the main platform has been raised and lengthened. The former locomen's messroom seen next to Whitby signalbox in the photograph on page 81 has been re-erected on the platform extension but the biggest visible change to Pickering Station is the North Eastern footbridge which was opened on 7 April 1997. It was acquired from Walker Gate, now on the Tyne & Wear Metro, at the same time as the bridge from neighbouring Howdon on Tyne, which was installed at Goathland in 1986.

In 1996 a new paint shop was added to the carriage works which occupies a site between the station and High Mill level crossing. The permanent way department shed at New Bridge should be finished during 1998. A major reconstruction of Pickering Station is still planned culminating in replacement of the overall roof, removed in 1952.

Since 1991 the Railway has advertised an all steam timetable with diesels reserved for emergency use and occasional specials. The 1998 service operates every day from 21 March to 1 November with between five and eight trains each way daily. Winter operation depends on permanent way work but in 1997 there was a service every Saturday and Sunday through November followed by Santa Specials then normal trains between Boxing Day and New Year.

At a time when many preserved railways have been reporting reduced traffic figures, the NYMR sold 280,766 tickets in 1996. The previous record had been 250,312 in 1990. The 1997 tally eased back to 269,857. The majority of ticket sales are of full line returns. Like most other lines, the NYMR seeks to maintain interest with better facilities and special events. It already offers a more comprehensive timetable than most other preserved lines. It needs to tap more effectively into the Whitby market. Ideally this means steam trains to Whitby but there are other possible methods involving better use of RRNE trains with a NYMR presence (ie office) at Whitby Station.

Stanier class 5 4-6-0T No. 44767 'George Stephenson' climbing past Darnholme on the way up to Goathland on 23 April 1988. *(G.W. Morrison)*

Levisham Station preserved.
The view towards Newtondale
Forest. *(John Bateman)*

2826 L. N. E. R. 2826
FOR CONDITIONS SEE BACK. Available for three days including day of issue
STAITHES to
KETTLENESS
Fare THIRD / S. 3507 \ 11d.C CLASS
KETTLENESS

0009 2nd- (3432 N) SPECIAL CHEAP SINGLE (3432 N) SPECIAL CHEAP SINGLE -2nd 0009
Guisborough to
Guisborough Thornaby — Guisborough Thornaby
THORNABY
(N) For conditions see over — (N) For conditions see over

0499 L. N. E. R. 0499
CHILD
FOR CONDITIONS SEE BACK. Available for three days, including day of issue
THORNTON DALE to
SCARBOROUGH
THIRD CLASS Fare 1s 4d.C

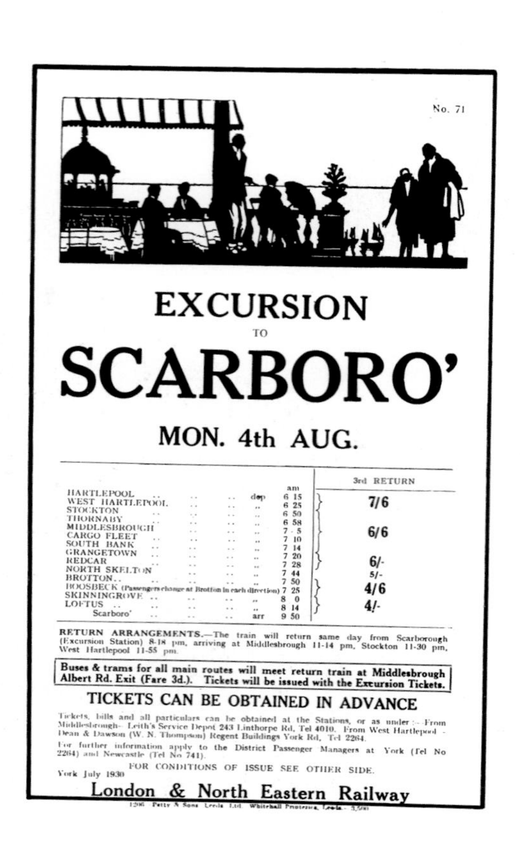

No. 71

EXCURSION
TO
SCARBORO'
MON. 4th AUG.

		am	3rd RETURN
HARTLEPOOL	dep	6 15	7/6
WEST HARTLEPOOL	..	6 25	
STOCKTON	..	6 50	
THORNABY	..	6 58	
MIDDLESBROUGH	..	7 5	6/6
CARGO FLEET	..	7 10	
SOUTH BANK	..	7 14	
GRANGETOWN	..	7 20	
REDCAR	..	7 28	6/-
NORTH SKELTON	..	7 44	5/-
BROTTON..	..	7 50	
BOOSBECK (Passengers change at Brotton in each direction)		7 25	4/6
SKINNINGROVE	..	8 0	
LOFTUS	..	8 14	4/-
Scarboro'	arr	9 50	

RETURN ARRANGEMENTS.—The train will return same day from Scarborough (Excursion Station) 8-18 pm, arriving at Middlesbrough 11-14 pm, Stockton 11-30 pm, West Hartlepool 11-55 pm.

Buses & trams for all main routes will meet return train at Middlesbrough Albert Rd. Exit (Fare 3d.). Tickets will be issued with the Excursion Tickets.

TICKETS CAN BE OBTAINED IN ADVANCE

Tickets, bills and all particulars can be obtained at the Stations, or as under :—From Middlesbrough—Leith's Service Depot 243 Linthorpe Rd, Tel 4010. From West Hartlepool - Dean & Dawson (W. N. Thompson) Regent Buildings York Rd, Tel 2264.

For further information apply to the District Passenger Managers at York (Tel No 2264) and Newcastle (Tel No 741).

FOR CONDITIONS OF ISSUE SEE OTHER SIDE.

York July 1930

London & North Eastern Railway

1296 Petty & Sons Leeds Ltd. Whitehall Printeries, Leeds—3,500

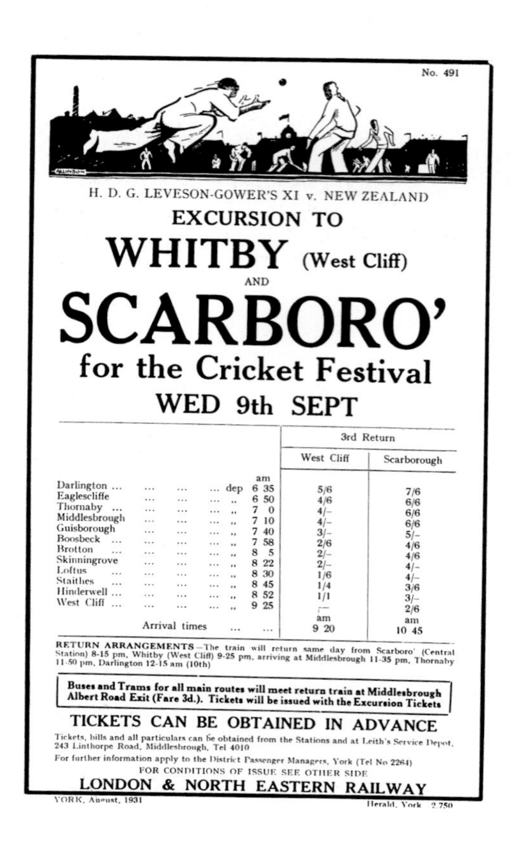

No. 491

H. D. G. LEVESON-GOWER'S XI v. NEW ZEALAND

EXCURSION TO
WHITBY (West Cliff)
AND
SCARBORO'
for the Cricket Festival
WED 9th SEPT

		am	3rd Return West Cliff	3rd Return Scarborough
Darlington ...	dep	6 35	5/6	7/6
Eaglescliffe	,,	6 50	4/6	6/6
Thornaby ...	,,	7 0	4/–	6/6
Middlesbrough	,,	7 10	4/–	6/6
Guisborough	,,	7 40	3/–	5/–
Boosbeck ...	,,	7 58	2/6	4/6
Brotton ...	,,	8 5	2/–	4/6
Skinningrove	,,	8 22	2/–	4/–
Loftus ...	,,	8 30	1/6	4/–
Staithes ...	,,	8 45	1/4	3/6
Hinderwell ...	,,	8 52	1/1	3/–
West Cliff ...	,,	9 25	—	2/6
Arrival times ...			am 9 20	am 10 45

RETURN ARRANGEMENTS.—The train will return same day from Scarboro' (Central Station) 8-15 pm, Whitby (West Cliff) 9-25 pm, arriving at Middlesbrough 11-35 pm, Thornaby 11-50 pm, Darlington 12-15 am (10th)

Buses and Trams for all main routes will meet return train at Middlesbrough Albert Road Exit (Fare 3d.). Tickets will be issued with the Excursion Tickets

TICKETS CAN BE OBTAINED IN ADVANCE

Tickets, bills and all particulars can be obtained from the Stations and at Leith's Service Depot, 243 Linthorpe Road, Middlesbrough, Tel 4010

For further information apply to the District Passenger Managers, York (Tel No 2264)

FOR CONDITIONS OF ISSUE SEE OTHER SIDE

LONDON & NORTH EASTERN RAILWAY

YORK, August, 1931 — Herald, York 2,750

Rights of Way

When closed lines were sold off for redevelopment, it was naturally more difficult to find buyers in the more remote areas. As much by accident as by intent, some stretches of track bed have survived as footpaths or cycle ways. Only in recent times has there been any concerted effort to develop dismantled railways for recreational use. This has come after many rights of way had already been destroyed.

One can cycle virtually the whole of the Scarborough to Whitby line from Gallows Close, near Falsgrave Tunnel, to the south end of Larpool Viaduct. The short missing bits at Scalby and Ravenscar are easily bypassed. Soon Larpool Viaduct itself is to be opened to cyclists.

Further north, a 2½ mile stretch of the Guisborough branch is available to walkers and cyclists from Nunthorpe Junction to a point east of Pinchinthorpe where the trail goes off into Guisborough Forest. There is no access at Nunthorpe Junction, only at Pinchinthorpe where both the original Stockton & Darlington and the 1877 North Eastern station houses survive on either side of the road bridge which replaced a level crossing in 1877.

You can walk, but not cycle, from Goathland to Grosmont, down the incline and along the Beck Hole branch. You can hear the trains battling up the nearby 1 in 49 on the 1865 alignment which made the incline redundant.

Another rope worked incline now available for walking is that on the Rosedale branch. This closed in 1929 but passes through such wild and remote territory that the track bed has never been redeveloped. Spectacular views can be enjoyed on a clear day. From Blakey Junction, you can observe the long sweep of the East Rosedale branch as it curves round the head of the valley towards its terminus which is now a farmyard above Hill Cottages.

The track bed can also be walked from Sandsend Station towards Kettleness Tunnel affording a taste of what it was like travelling this scenic coastal line.

Tackling the 1 in 41 up from Staintondale to Ravenscar.
(Martin Bairstow)

During the Summers of 1908 to 1914, Beck Hole could be visited by 'autocar' (NER push-pull train). Today we can walk the branch.
(Lens of Sutton)

Integrated Transport?

The situation is so familiar. Malton rail and bus stations are adjacent. Departures to Pickering are .05 past the hour with four journeys per day going through to Whitby. Train arrivals are on the odd hour when coming from Blackpool but at .07 past the even hour, two minutes after the bus goes, when the train is from Liverpool.

Suppose I want to go from Leeds to Whitby. I have four options:

(1) Train at 8.52 changing at Middlesbrough. Overall journey time 3 hours 6 minutes. The tight seven minute connection will normally be held in the event of modest late running. The fare will reflect the involuntary excess mileage.

(2) Through bus at 9.20 taking 3 hours 8 minutes – a bit uncomfortable – no loo and I can't read without feeling dizzy.

(3) 10.07 train changing onto bus at Malton. Overall journey time 2 hours 21 minutes. This is actually five minutes quicker than by the 9.45 Saturdays only through train shown in my summer 1964 timetable. Problem – I must gather the information from different sources, I can't book a through ticket and the connection will not wait.

(4) Decide the whole thing is too complicated and go by car.

The only serious hope of weaning me away from my car must be the rail/bus change at Malton. But does anybody do it? They certainly would if it were a train connection. This is not because they're all enthusiasts. It is more that one could depend on certain conditions which seem never to have applied to bus connections.

(1) It would be shown in the same timetable as the train to Malton. Information and through tickets could be obtained from any staffed station or agency in the country.

(2) There would be a reasonable chance of the connection being held in the event of late running. If there were a serious delay, the Train Operating Company would accept responsibility for getting you there somehow.

(3) There would be no difficulty finding the connection even if there was nobody to ask, station platforms being more substantial and recognisable than a bus stop. The conductor on the first train would probably announce the connection.

(4) In short there would be a degree of confidence.

It seems so obvious that if these conditions extended to the bus, then there could easily be a standard of service superior to that which was seen even when the direct railway was in operation.

The bus is operated by Yorkshire Coastliner, which is associated with Prism Rail, the holder of four rail franchises. They should have as much expertise in the matter as do Regional Railways North East. Both know that much of their revenue is derived from the 'network effect' – taking a proportion of the fares paid by longer distance passengers using a variety of operators.

What we don't want is a 'one off' special arrangement which costs more in printing advertising leaflets than the gross revenue earned only to be withdrawn after a few months. What is needed is a national network of strategic bus routes linking into the railway system in much the way that the various train operating companies do business with each other. Almost all the buses in this network would comprise services already in operation, which would continue to carry their own indigenous traffic as well as being available to longer distance travellers with rail tickets.

It is what the Rail Regulator calls a seamless journey. It is what was promised when the local trains were withdrawn more than thirty years ago. It is so obvious. It would cost next to nothing to implement. Why doesn't it happen?

Never the twain shall meet? Departing Malton for Whitby. SBW30 in 1957, 41251 in 1962.
(J. C. W. Halliday, David Beeken)

7357 L. N. E. R.
FOR CONDITIONS SEE BACK. Available for three days, including day of issue.
WHITBY, WEST CLIFF to
HINDERWELL
Fare S 1s. 4d.C
THIRD 3591 CLASS
HINDERWELL

0314 2nd- SPECIAL CHEAP SINGLE SPECIAL CHEAP SINGLE -2nd
Castleton (Yorks.) to
Castleton (Yorks.) Nunthorpe Castleton (Yorks.) Nunthorpe
NUNTHORPE
(N) (N)
For conditions see over For conditions see over

0229 2nd- SPECIAL CHEAP SINGLE SPECIAL CHEAP SINGLE -2nd
Boosbeck to
Boosbeck Loftus Boosbeck Loftus
LOFTUS
(N) (N)
For conditions see over For conditions see over

Conclusion

In the first (1989) edition of this book, I described the simultaneous closure of the Malton and Scarborough to Whitby lines as 'one of the more savage excesses' of the Beeching Period. Particularly in the light of research for Volume Two, I think this comment ought to be moderated. In the context of mid 1960s transport policy, Whitby was perhaps lucky to retain even one of its three rail outlets. On the evidence then available and on the statutory criterion of hardship to regular users, the Esk Valley was the correct line to be singled out for retention.

This is not to deny that the decision was reached with indecent haste in circumstances, which would have been inconceivable at any period before, or since. It is a pity that the Malton to Whitby route could not have survived to take its place as a feeder to today's Trans Pennine and Inter City network. If it had, perhaps the North Yorkshire Moors Railway would have preserved part of the Scarborough line instead.

There remains much interest in the Whitby area: the scenic Esk Valley Line, a leading preserved railway, heavy freight movement north of Boulby, an exhilarating 20 mile bike ride and plenty of history which I have tried to bring to life in these two volumes.

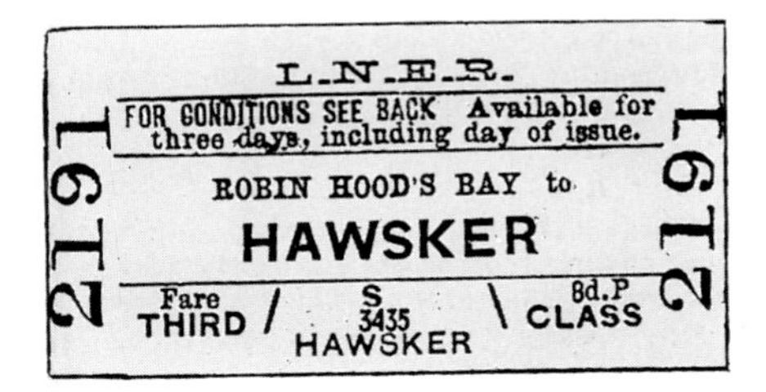

HOW IT MIGHT HAVE BEEN. Although the class 150/2 'Sprinter' units were only a stop gap solution on the Scarborough – Liverpool service, they would have sufficed for the Whitby connection. 150251 approaching Malton on 3 October 1987.
(John Bateman)

HOW IT WAS. By August 1968, the track had been lifted through Scalby Station. Today the site is a housing estate.
(D. Butterfield)

Appendices

The Whitby & Pickering Railway

Opened	
Whitby – Grosmont	15. 5.1835
Grosmont – Pickering	26. 5.1836
Pickering – Malton	7. 7.1845
Closed to passengers	
Grosmont – Beck Hole	21. 9.1914
Grosmont – Malton	6. 3.1965
Closed to all traffic	
Grosmont – Beck Hole	1951
Grosmont – Pickering	6. 3.1965
Pickering – Rillington	1. 7.1966
Reopened	
Grosmont – Pickering	22. 4.1973

miles	Stations	opened	closed
0	Whitby Town	15. 5.1835	–
1½	Ruswarp	15. 5.1835	–
3	Sleights	15. 5.1835	–
6¼	Grosmont	15. 5.1835	–
–	Beck Hole	26. 5.1836	21. 9.1914
9½	Goathland	26. 5.1836	6. 3.1965
15	Newtondale	13. 4.1981	–
18	Levisham	26. 5.1836	6. 3.1965
24	Pickering	26. 5.1836	6. 3.1965
27½	Marishes Road	7. 7.1845	6. 3.1965
30½	Rillington	7. 7.1845	20. 9.1930
35	Malton	7. 7.1845	–

The new route between Deviation Junction (Grosmont) and Goathland Summit opened on 1.7.1865 and the old route was abandoned south of Beck Hole. A summer only passenger service was restored between Grosmont and Beck Hole in 1908. Goathland Station was resited when the deviation opened in 1865. Goathland, Levisham and Pickering stations reopened on 22.4.1973 though Pickering was on a temporary site until 24.5.1975.

Scarborough – Whitby – Saltburn

Opened	
Loftus – Skinningrove (goods)	27. 5.1867
Skinningrove – Brotton (goods)	21. 4.1865
Brotton – Saltburn (goods)	1. 7.1872
Loftus – Saltburn (passenger)	1. 4.1875
Whitby Town – Loftus	3.12.1883
Scarborough – Prospect Hill Jn	16. 7.1885
Closed to passengers	
Brotton – Saltburn	6. 9.1957
Whitby West Cliff – Loftus	3. 5.1958
Loftus – Brotton	30. 4.1960
Prospect Hill Jn – West Cliff	10. 6.1961
Scarborough – Whitby Town	6. 3.1965
Closed to all traffic	
Whitby West Cliff – Loftus	3. 5.1958
Prospect Hill Jn – West Cliff	10. 6.1961
Loftus – Skinningrove	10. 8.1963
Gallows Close – Whitby Town	6. 3.1965
Falsgrave Jn – Gallows Close	1981
Reopened	
Skinningrove – Boulby	1. 4.1974

miles	Stations	opened	closed
0	Scarborough Central	7. 7.1845	–
2¾	Scalby	16. 7.1885	28. 2.1953
5	Cloughton	16. 7.1885	6. 3.1965
7	Hayburn Wyke	16. 7.1885	6. 3.1965
8	Stainton Dale	16. 7.1885	6. 3.1965
10¼	Ravenscar	16. 7.1885	6. 3.1965
13½	Fyling Hall	16. 7.1885	6. 3.1965
15¼	Robin Hood's Bay	16. 7.1885	6. 3.1965
18½	Hawsker	16. 7.1885	6. 3.1965
–	Whitby Town	15. 5.1835	–
21¾	Whitby West Cliff	3.12.1883	10. 6.1961
23¾	Sandsend	3.12.1883	3. 5.1958
26¾	Kettleness	3.12.1883	3. 5.1958
30	Hinderwell	3.12.1883	3. 5.1958
31¾	Staithes	3.12.1883	3. 5.1958
35¼	Grinkle	3.12.1883	10. 9.1939
36½	Loftus	1. 4.1875	30. 4.1960
37½	Skinningrove	1. 4.1875	28. 6.1952
41¼	Brotton	1. 4.1875	30. 4.1960
42¾	North Skelton	1902	8. 9.1951
45½	Saltburn	17. 8.1861	–

Middlesbrough – Guisborough – Esk Valley – Whitby

Opened	
Grosmont – Whitby	15. 5.1835
Middlesbrough – Guisborough (goods)	11.11.1853
Middlesbrough – Guisborough (passenger)	25. 2.1854
Picton – Stokesley	3. 3.1857
Stokesley – Ingleby (goods)	1. 2.1858
Ingleby – Kildale (goods)	6. 4.1858
Battersby – West Rosedale (goods)	27. 3.1861
Kildale – Castleton (goods)	1. 4.1861
Stokesley – Castleton (passenger)	1. 4.1861
Guisborough – Boosbeck (goods)	1862
Boosbeck – Brotton (goods)	23. 2.1865
Brotton – Skinningrove (goods)	Apr 1865
Blakey Jn – East Rosedale (goods)	18. 8.1865
Castleton – Grosmont	2.10.1865
Skinningrove – Loftus (goods)	27. 5.1867
Brotton – Loftus (passenger)	1. 4.1875
Guisborough – Brotton (passenger)	1.11.1878
Closed to passengers	
Picton – Battersby	12. 6.1954
Guisborough – Loftus	30. 4.1960
Nunthorpe – Guisborough	29. 2.1964
Closed to all traffic	
Battersby – West and East Rosedale	24. 1.1929
Picton – Stokesley	29.11.1958
Guisborough – Boosbeck	30. 4.1960
Skinningrove – Loftus	10. 8.1963
Boosbeck – Brotton	12. 9.1964
Stokesley – Battersby	31. 7.1965

miles	miles	Stations	opened	closed
0		Middlesbrough	27.12.1830	–
3		Ormesby (Marton)	25. 2.1854	–
4		Gypsy Lane	3. 5.1976	–
4½		Nunthorpe	25. 2.1854	–
	7½	Pinchinthorpe	25. 2.1854	27.10.1951
	8¾	Hutton Gate	1. 1.1904	29. 2.1964
	10	Guisborough	25. 2.1854	29. 2.1964
	14	Boosbeck	1.11.1878	30. 4.1960
	16¾	Brotton	1. 4.1875	30. 4.1960
	18½	Skinningrove	1. 4.1875	28. 6.1952
	19½	Loftus	1. 4.1875	30. 4.1960
8¼		Great Ayton	1. 4.1868	–
	0	Picton	2. 6.1852	2. 1.1960
	2	Trenholme Bar	3. 3.1857	12. 6.1954
	4¼	Potto	3. 3.1857	12. 6.1954
	5¼	Sexhow	3. 3.1857	12. 6.1954
	8½	Stokesley	3. 3.1857	12. 6.1954
	11½	Ingleby	1. 4.1861	12. 6.1954
11	12	Battersby	1. 4.1861	–
12¾		Kildale	1. 4.1861	–
16¾		Commondale	1. 4.1861	–
18½		Castleton Moor	1. 4.1861	–
19¾		Danby	2.10.1865	–
23½		Lealholm	2.10.1865	–
25½		Glaisdale	2.10.1865	–
27¼		Egton	2.10.1865	–
28¾		Grosmont	15. 5.1835	–
32		Sleights	15. 5.1835	–
33½		Ruswarp	15. 5.1835	–
35		Whitby Town	15. 5.1835	–